Diana
Memory of a Rose

JUNE MENDOZA

A personal reminiscence
By Susan Maxwell Skinner

Photographs by Anwar Hussein

"We taught the world new ways to dream."*

Contents

*Quote from Sunset Boulevard, by Andrew Lloyd Webber

To order books by Susan Maxwell Skinner:
Contact Betty Milner Productions, 3229 Deodar Street, Carmichael, CA 95608 (916) 481-0334 Email: Sknrband@aol.com

Leading Lady. Diana's life was a theatrical pageant; her story like a pop musical. Here she attends the opening of *The Phantom of the Opera*. The tale must have struck a chord. Diana saw Phantom a dozen times. RIGHT: *Hello my friend.* A superstar lionized by celebrities, 24-year-old Diana is serenaded by singer Neil Diamond at the '85 White House gala.

CHAPTER ONE

The Overture

"One minute I was a nobody. The next minute,
I was the Princess of Wales."

— DIANA, IN A 1995 INTERVIEW

Some societies believe you die twice. The first time is when your heart stops. The second—and truly fatal time—is when everyone who remembers you is gone. Then you are merely a name in history.

In the case of Princess Diana, this will take time. The era she inhabited was self-indulgent; people liked their fantasies pre-packaged and lived their lives through her. The Diana story was a lavish pop opera for almost two decades. Nearly everyone felt they knew her. Now, years after her death, her face and smile fan a flame more enduring than singer Elton John's candle. I recently met a Californian nine-year-old who keeps a voluminous scrapbook on Diana. She barely remembers The Funeral. It seems generation after generation wants to keep this fabled princess around. Her smile—delivered as faithfully in death as in life—still comforts. It comforts me to know that though her life was short and often exasperating, she made a difference. Apparently, she mattered.

I will not try to analyze the whole Diana phenomenon. She simply mattered to me.

I was one of those who promoted her path towards Ultimate Pop Heroine. Part of her accredited press corps, I wore a badge and dogged her steps for eight years. We chronicled everything we saw. Nothing was too trivial. Academics and highbrows sneered that we pandered to the most vicarious of public obsessions. Maybe. But nobody could fault our diligence. We untiringly kept the Diana market fed. I doubt we foresaw her as the second most influential woman in history[1]. We hardly considered that an increasingly godless society was replacing its divinities with celebrities like Diana. We were not paid to think. We just did our jobs.

How ironic those academics now have hacks like us to thank for mountains of information on a person they will go on dissecting—even after her 'second death'—as they do Julius Caesar or Napoleon Bonaparte. Dianaology research will take place not in university libraries but in the archives of the popular press, where a pop princess belongs.

We could never be bosom pals or confidantes to a princess. But though we were often yelled at for blocking real people's view of the star, we were there with her compliance. It was a professional symbiosis. She provided us with a living. We gave her the publicity she needed. I liked her and she was pleasant to me.

Diana was a 19-year-old fiancée when I left my native New Zealand for England. The Wedding of the Century assignment was a high point of my career. Afterwards, I stayed on in London. Buckingham Palace became my beat. As a naïve new girl from the Colonies, I felt that I grew up with Diana. I was seven years her senior

1. I give the Holy Mother that distinction.

Countries shared their most breath-taking panoramas with The Waleses. Central Australia's Ayers Rock riveted the royals. INSERT: Author Susan Maxwell Skinner and photographer Anwar Hussein boggled, too. RIGHT: Different strokes...a Venetian gondola is oceans apart from a Maori war canoe in New Zealand. FAR RIGHT: A biblical Diana outraged some viewers at Liverpool Tate Gallery. But Luigi Baggi's wooden statue portrays elevation of celebrity to divinity by an increasingly godless society.

but we were hurled into the shark pond at the same time. We learned the survival game and wore its scars. Neither of us had it too easy. I probably cried as much over my personal life as she did for hers. I discovered later that we had the same eating disorder.

But I can never regret my Diana years. Her life was a pageant and, on her coat tails, I saw the same dazzling panoramas. The first time I boggled at Ayers Rock, Botticelli's *Venus* or a Venetian sunset was Diana's first view of these wonders, too. I beheld the spectacle of tattooed, chanting Maori warriors shipping their delicate royal guest across a harbor by massive war canoe. I saw ballets performed for her delight. I stood nearby as she launched the world's costliest passenger liner and caught her bubbling excitement. I was a bit-player, often reminding myself that her life was not some movie with a cast of thousands. Diana was real, a woman–though barely much more than a child–for whom the eager world exhibited its proudest spectacles. Nothing was too much effort to enchant one more smile out of the Princess of Wales.

At the start of Diana's career, most of the press pack was considerably older than the ingénue. Though some felt they were Hemingway-reincarnate, they never wondered if recording the life of a Northamptonshire lass was a grown-up job. We never pondered what any 19-year-old had done worth chronicling for posterity. Oh yes, she had kept her virginity for a length of time rare in the 80s. Otherwise, she had done little more than blush and simper and become engaged to a 32-going-on-60-year-old Prince Charles.

Yet there she was and there we were, cameras and note-

DEMETZ STUDIO, ITALY.

ABOVE: Performing *Coppelia*,
New Zealand dancers remind
Diana of a childhood yearning to
be a ballerina. BELOW: In a world
hooked on celebrity, the
masses thrilled to a royal who,
even in unguarded moments,
photographed like a supermodel.

books poised. Everything Diana did was newsworthy. If she lunched, we reported what she ate. If she did not eat, we recorded that, too. If such a fishbowl existence was enough to put her off eating, we never considered her confusion. Years later, she said "(people) hung on my every word. The problem was, I didn't have any..."

No problem. If she were mute, we recorded the silent-star eloquence of her facial expressions. Or we wrote about her clothes. Voluminously. I knew the designer of everything she wore. I remember slavishly reading a double-page spread on Diana's socks. One day, Diana styled her hair in a French twist. At the time, there were 11 national daily newspapers in Britain. The news that a 22-year-old had changed her hairstyle was on the front page of every one, including the sensible broadsheets. Alas, Queen Elizabeth, Diana's mama-in-law, made an important speech that day. Her utterances were upstaged. Blaming Diana for the slight, the Monarch missed the real warning. Society was changing. As Paul McCartney had said: "Not for better but for always..."

The Queen had given her life to service. But noble royal traditions could not compete with the tide of pop culture that took hold of the 80s. Hooked on Celebrity, the masses preferred an icon who photographed like a super-model, who reached out, touched, cried and confessed. They rejoiced in the first royal mum who admitted hugging her boys "to death"; who patron-ized fast food outlets with Windsor princes in tow. A mid-brow who sobbed through a dozen performances of Phantom of the Opera was endearingly in tune with the mainstream. In fact, Diana's saga might have been an Andrew Lloyd Webber weepy. What a circus, what a show! What costumes! What a run: 16 dazzling years before the final curtain. And even then, the reviews would continue for years.

While her in-laws gnashed their teeth, the Pop Princess became central to the fantasies of generations of ordinary people. The more accessible she appeared, the more remote the Windsors seemed. The more emotion she displayed, the more frigid they looked. The more glamorous her clothes, the drabber theirs. They were corset-bound; she was pneumatic, athletic, strid-ing on racehorse legs.

After centuries of pedigree livestock and heirs, the Spencers of Althorp accidentally[1] bred the ultimate package. When 21-year-old Diana leaped up

---

1. She was the third daughter of an earl and countess who desperately needed a viscount.

Years after Diana's death, people still find reassurance in her smile. Her father said: "Diana has a sympathetic face ...the kind you can't help but trust."

from a convertible and caught a bouquet mid-air in Sydney, her press officer, Vic Chapman, laughed and told me: "The girl has everything. No, she is everything..." In truth, she had only to be herself.

She was no scholar. At Althorp, her brother showed me Diana's final school report. Dismal stuff, it was, too. Charles Spencer had nicknamed his sister 'Brian'–after a slow-witted snail on a children's TV show - and her mathematics teacher was no kinder. Next to the pathetic test score of 17 per cent, the teacher wrote: "Diana Spencer will never understand numbers." Diana blamed herself for her parents' scandalous divorce. She never forgot cowering on a staircase and hearing her mother driven away, forever. She suffered all through her school years. Said her piano teacher: "The staff knew she was struggling...she was distracted by the awful torment in her family at the time." Her Latin teacher's report card said: "A poor memory greatly reduces her output." In West Heath School, Kent, you can see Diana's endorsement of the most costly education Spencer money could buy. Tooled in a wooden locker are the words: "Diana Spencer was here in this cupbord (sic)." We can only guess at what demon she escaped in the cupboard. Her spelling teacher, perhaps?

In his funeral eulogy, Earl Spencer summed up his sister: "A very insecure person at heart, almost childlike in her desire to do good...so she could release herself from deep feelings of unworthiness." Even her dresser had passed more school examinations than the woman whose sumptuous clothes she ironed. Little wonder Diana thought of herself as "hopeless, a dropout. I wasn't good at anything."

TOP: Diana-fever grips Sydney. During the six-week '83 tour, one fifth of Australia's population turned out for a 'gecko' at the 21-year-old mum. **LEFT:** In sailor hat, an excited princess launches P&O's ocean liner *Royal Princess*.

But what global presence this least promising of the Spencer brood would eventually gain. By the age of 23, Diana could enter a White House salon–which the First Couple had packed with a dream-team of famous Americans–and know not only was she the biggest star there, but that superstars like John Travolta and Neil Diamond would fall over their feet to schmooze her. In Canada, I spoke to Prime Minster Pierre Trudeau and he sighed: "Why don't you ask me about the Princess' beautiful eyes?" Movie star Tom Cruise threw a hissy fit when told his mum could not join a VIP lineup to meet Diana. Tenor Luciano Pavarotti dedicated arias to her. General Colin Powell was at pains to brag about being (distantly) related to her. Mother Theresa of Calcutta praised her "beautiful spirit." Every milestone in her career was celebrated by postage stamps. Some issued by countries she probably could not locate on a map.

By her 30s, Diana could take a microphone and deliver compelling speeches to assemblies studded with luminaries such as diplomat Henry Kissinger and broadcaster Barbara Walters. This was the girl who refused speaking parts in school plays and loathed anyone quoting her. Yet she

remained a strange dichotomy, capable of both steely strength and aching vulnerability. Her contradictions became as natural as breathing for most of us. We accepted her, gloveless, embracing lepers. Equally, we approved her designer threads and golf-ball sapphires. We justified her capriciousness and her love affairs, thus forgiving our own weaknesses. She proved you did not need to be saintly to leave the world a better place.

As Charles Spencer said, there was no point in canonizing Diana. She stood "tall enough as a human being of unique qualities not to need to be seen as a saint."

A humanitarian activist who lived in a palace and championed the downtrodden (changing the world while wearing Armani pants) seems contradictory. But the Princess' People never thought about it. We were as accepting of her idiosyncrasies as we were accustomed to her film-star face. After all, she was the biggest star civilization had seen and there were no precedents for her to observe. Nor for us to expect. There was only one of her kind.

David Hankinson, who painted one of 13 official portraits during Diana's 16-year reign over global consciousness, said: "Aged 19 she was catapulted into public life and she created Diana. She created herself. No one helped her."

ABOVE: A modern-day icon and the original love goddess. Diana meets Botticelli's *Venus* **in Florence. RIGHT: Polka dot socks worn to a polo match sent press coverage of her husband's sporting prowess to the cutting-room floor.**

A kiss is just a kiss. The Buckingham Palace balcony vignette convinced Neo Romantics of a royal love-match. RIGHT: Later in '81, the newly-weds set up house—and nursery—at Kensington Palace. OPPOSITE: In Britain and in many less likely outposts, stamps celebrated the Wedding of the Century. *Stamps from the author's collection.*

S.M.S.

CHAPTER TWO

The First Act

"My first screen Kiss!"

—DIANA, RETIRING FROM BUCKINGHAM PALACE BALCONY, 1981.

It was the most bittersweet anniversary–July 29, 2001–Diana and Charles' twentieth.

For a start, the couple was divorced in 1996 and worse, the bride had been dead almost four years. Still, the Wedding of the Century was an unforgettable milestone. It had been the most romantic event of the modern era and we felt compelled to commemorate it.

A church ceremony to join two lives had the toes of the world tingling. Still an ingénue, Diana was stunned by the national and worldwide fixation. Barbara Daly, her makeup artist, told me: "Diana and I watched the incredible crowds on TV at 6:30am on the wedding day. She kept saying–'look at all the people, I can't believe it.' She was quite humble. She was amazed at the big fuss for the wedding of one girl."

It was a State Occasion, with an excess of monarchs, prime ministers and presidents all hugger-mugger in St Paul's Cathedral, London. Television lighting in every inch of the church created makeup challenges. "The object was not to lose sight of the fact that she was only 19 years old," Barbara Daly explained. "The joy of her being so young was her fresh loveliness. I didn't want to make her look older. I was amazed at how happy and calm she was before the wedding. Calmer than anyone else around her. She was getting married to the man she loved." Everyone was looking their best. Nancy Reagan hit town with a peach Galliano wedding ensemble and strict instructions from her husband to shake any proffered royal hand but "under no circumstances curtsey."

As a court correspondent for a Commonwealth newspaper, I had been curtseying on and off to royalty for years. Two days before the wedding, Prince Charles spotted me sitting on the grass at a polo match. "Don't I know you from New Zealand?" he asked. "Are you coming to my wedding?" Rising to my knees, I asked if he and Lady Diana were looking forward to the big day. "Immensely," he replied. "Mostly looking forward to getting away afterwards. I must say, you do look rather strange talking to me on your knees," he laughed. "But I suppose it's quite appropriate, ha, ha, ha!"

I was less conspicuous at St Paul's. Tucked away, I clutched a $US60 dollar press pass and my yellow Panama hat. It was a copy of one of Diana's and certainly not the silliest hat in St Paul's. I think Maori soprano Kiri Te Kanawa, the soloist, took that prize. It was a silly time in general. Street parties were planned all over Britain. London was a rainbow of bunting. Photographer Lord Snowdon's portrait of Diana's face beamed from postage stamps and tea towels. I rose at 5 am to pick my way down the Mall, through a maze of sleeping Londoners. On waking, they regained the ebullience of the previous night, when the whole Mall echoed with *'oh my darling Lady Di'*. People cheered mounted policemen. They even cheered the men shoveling horse manure.

Like everyone watching the spectacle, I felt that July 29, 1981–like the Moon Landing–would be one of those yardstick events in my life. Of course, 16 years later, fate would make a graver church procession–with Diana again in the central vehicle–even more epoch-making. But who could see that far ahead? London was in the mood for love and the bride had somehow turned the world's heart to mush. It was hailed as the dawn of the Neo Romantic age. At St Paul's, we were drugged by the smell of thousands of white roses.

Even deep in the cathedral, the babbling, sardine-packed throngs outside were audible. Suddenly there was a hush and a thousand-throat gasp as Cinderella stepped from her carriage. We all held our breath watching Diana support her ill and doddering father, the late Earl Johnny Spencer, up the aisle. I saw her as tall, pale and lovely. Lip-readers later deciphered her royal fiancé's greeting at the altar.

Charles (kneeling): "You look lovely."
Diana (blushing): "Lovely for you."

I had met her at the polo a few days before. She was in jeans. A gamin. Now in the massive ivory Emanuel gown, she was a princess. I saw the gown 17 years later in Northamptonshire, where it is part of the Diana museum at the Spencer family seat of Althorp. Though faded, it still makes observers blubber.

Towards the end of her life, Diana had become jaded about The Dress and the broken promises it symbolized. A friend, fashion entrepreneur Roberto Devorik, asked where she kept it. Diana replied: "It's in a cupboard. I hope the moths eat it a bit and reduce the volume." But in 1981, no one thought The Dress over the top. For Neo Romantics, the bouffant crinoline was perfect. Married designers David and Elizabeth Emanuel were the fashion dream team. Elizabeth recently said: "We had no idea Diana would choose us. One day I picked up the phone and it was Diana. She said, 'would you do me the honor of making my wedding dress?' She was sweet and shy and a little bit chubby. We wanted to make the most wonderful dress of all time for her."

OPPOSITE PAGE, TOP: The bride trails a 25ft train into St Paul's Cathedral.
LOWER LEFT: Designer David Emanuel fluffs Diana's veil before the long walk to the altar with her ailing father, Lord 'Johnny' Spencer.
ABOVE AND NEXT PAGE: The Prince and Princess of Wales face two million Londoners and a television audience of 750 million.
BELOW: An African postage stamp recalls the honeymooners' flight to Gibraltar.

Elizabeth and Diana scoured the annals of royal brides, wanting to outdo them all.

"We found out which dress had the longest train," said Elizabeth. "She said: 'Okay, it's got to be longer than that'." The bill for such extravagance was a token 1000 guineas, paid by Diana's mother. By tradition, the design had to be secret. Only after Diana's coach rattled from Clarence House did the Palace press office issue details as voluminous as the gown itself. I heard a bewildered CBS anchorman snarling, "what the hell's a crinoline?" and I wondered why CBS had sent a man on a woman's job.

Despite much devious presspionage, the Emanuels managed to keep the biggest secret since D-Day. During three months of stitching, the couturiers code-named their client Deborah Smythson Wells. They locked fabric scraps away at night. "We used 42 yards of ivory silk taffeta," remembers Elizabeth. "Towards the end, fittings had to be relocated from our studio to the Palace because that was the only place large enough for the train. I remember Diana standing in Princess Anne's bedroom, her train spilling into the corridor."

The tight bodice had also been a work in progress. Its waist was 29 inches at the first fitting. Now it was 23 inches and still shrinking. Diana spotting had been a media sport all summer and I saw her in Bond St two days before the nuptials. The buxom girl of the engagement pictures was now a wafer. Tabloid headlines wailed: *We love you Di but don't get any thinner!* Elizabeth Emanuel was aware of Diana's stress. "She needed a lot of reassurance...she was, after all, so young."

No one who saw Diana in St Paul's suspected the turmoil she later described to biographer Andrew Morton. Her bulimia rampant, she had raided the Queen Mum's pantry on the wedding eve and made herself "sick as a parrot." Frantic the next morning that altar microphones might broadcast a growling stomach, she ate a decent breakfast before wallowing in the bath and contemplating "the most emotionally confusing day of my life." Her sisters, Sarah and Jane, laughed away her qualms about marriage. "Your face is on the tea towels, Duch,"[1] they crowed. "It's too late to chicken out."

Makeup lady Barbara Daly was in Diana's face from sunrise and she gave a different account of the bride's emotional state. "I was amazed at how happy and calm she was. Calmer than any of us. She was marrying the man she loved." Diana's hairdresser, Kevin Shanley, had similar memories. He told me he found Diana "had pulled out her heated rollers on one side and was happily talking to Prince Charles on the phone."

More than 750 million television viewers were unaware of a last-minute crisis at Clarence House. The Emanuels panicked when their massive gown barely fit into the tiny glass wedding coach with a tall bride and her even taller sire. The train, the crinoline and its 328ft tulle petticoat were cruelly crushed. But Earl Spencer later recalled how, cocooned in silk, he and Diana buoyed each other along the procession route.

"More people here," said Earl Spencer, "than at Wembley stadium."
"Oh Daddy, when were you ever at Wembley Stadium?"
"Hmmm...actually, never."

Elizabeth Emanuel watched Diana alight at the cathedral. "As she stepped out of the carriage, it looked to some as though the dress was a mass of creases. I said to my husband, oh God, it's all creased! He said the creases would fall out as she walked up the steps. Thankfully, they did." In the vestibule, David Emanuel fluffed up the veil. Seeing the entire Royal Family arrive at St Paul's had terrified him. "But when I saw Diana's face and realized how happy she was, I was fine," he said. Elizabeth straightened the train "to be sure it would line up properly as she walked up the aisle. Then we hurried to our seats. We were overwhelmed," she told me. "The world was watching and the bride looked so fabulous."

---

1. From childhood, Diana had been knick-named Duch, short for Duchess.

A kiss is still a kiss. But after years of posed or unposed smooching, displays of affection between Charles and Diana occur less and less. BELOW: By the '92 Korean tour, the pair hardly make eye contact. Divorce is the next destination. Diana later quipped: "I kissed a prince and he turned into a frog."

Minutes later, The Wedding was off to a magnificent, musical start with *Pomp and Circumstance* and trilling choirboys. I remember thinking that although the universe shared this magic, the ceremony felt intimate. We could not forget that this was a young girl marrying her sweetheart. Even the vows were a personalized event. Unlike Princess Anne, the Queen and even imperious Queen Victoria, Diana had refused 'to obey' in her pledges. The Archbishop of Canterbury approved. "It's bad to start your marriage with a downright lie," he said. Soon we heard a nervous Diana muff her husband's names and almost marry Philip Charles Arthur George. Barbara Daly told me Diana later confessed: "I think I got his name wrong back there. Do you think anyone noticed?" Just 750 million of us, Diana. It was hard not to love anyone so ingenuous about her stardom.

And everyone sympathized with the bride when her groom apparently sought his mother's permission to kiss on the palace balcony. Standing inside, Elizabeth Emanuel watched the newly-weds in silhouette. "When they kissed, it seemed like the world went mad. I remember it seemed like the whole world was smiling."

I learned later that a splitting headache - from her first all-day stint in a tiara - marred Diana's wedding day. Years later she complained to a friend about the occupational hazard of weighty diamond tiaras "which leave the head sore..."

By the time the Waleses left on honeymoon, I was on the Victoria Monument opposite Buckingham Palace, marooned by a sea of singing well-wishers. They had changed their song to *'oh my darling Princess Di'*. Typically, the bride telephoned the Emanuels from her honeymoon hide-away that night. "She thanked us for making her dress and making her feel so beautiful," Elizabeth Emanuel told me.

A couple of days later, I watched the royal yacht Britannia ease into the Mediterranean from Gibraltar. Rod Stewart's *We are Sailing* filled the straits and it seemed everyone was screaming like the Barbary apes on the Rock. Diana snuggled into her husband's arm and sobbed. They would be alone at last. With the 270-man Britannia crew.

We did not see them again till they berthed at Port Said to give a dinner party for President and Madame Sadat, of Egypt. Weeks later, as the couple continued honeymooning in Scotland, President Sadat was assassinated. A sympathy letter to Madame Sadat was just part of Diana's correspondence. She and Charles penned 6000 thank-you notes for wedding presents. I saw most of these at St James Palace. They ranged from knitted bed socks to a mountain of jewels (more than $1.8 million worth from Saudi royals alone), provoking Diana's exclamation: "Gosh, I'm becoming a very rich lady." Most valuable object was a 2ft solid gold, diamond-studded dhow from the ruler of Bahrain. Like Britannia, the vessel was no love boat. Stolen from Diana's apartment in the confusion following her death, it would become the center of a bitter scandal.

Long before then, we all knew the riches of the world could not have blessed the union. The arranged marriage paired two needy people with the partner least likely to comfort their insecurities. At polo less than a year after the wedding, I heard Prince Charles bark at cameramen: "Why don't you leave my bloody wife alone?" Hardly an endearment, I thought, for his heavily pregnant bride. It seemed the honeymoon was over.

The Archbishop of Canterbury called The Wedding of the Century "the stuff of fairytales." In 1996, a Decree Absolute officially ended a marriage that had been in its death-throes for years. By then, even the Neo Romantics agreed that fairytales are often pretty Grimm affairs. The 90s had also been ruthless with many of those who had packed St Paul's. Princess Grace was dead. Princess Anne was divorced. Prince Andrew, divorced. Lord Snowdon, divorced. David and Elizabeth Emanuel, divorced. Even opera singer Kiri Te Kanawa, whose angelic voice soared to the heights of St Paul's, divorced.

Sixteen years after the Wedding of the Century, Diana's magical glass coach was replaced by a gun carriage bearing her coffin. The only glass was a window in its lid. And her ivory wedding dress—that most wonderful dress of all time—now fades to a deeper shade of *café au lait* each summer at Althorp.

TOP: A voyage in the royal yacht Britannia was farewelled at Gibraltar and sailed inexorably to far nastier rocks. But the Mediterranean cruise was at least a security triumph. The honeymooners avoided cameras for two weeks. BOTTOM: They berthed at last at Port Said, Egypt. OPPOSITE: Still honeymooning, Diana favors photographer Anwar Hussein with a coy smile in Scotland.

CHAPTER THREE

The Child Players

"Remember, it's my job to be a mother..."
—DIANA, TO A PHOTOGRAPHER, 1983.

I waited in the blinding heat of Alice Springs, in March 1983. The Queen's Flight had just delivered the Waleses to the starting point of Diana's first Commonwealth tour. She seemed even younger than her 21 years. I saw the pale, round-shouldered girl among the ruddy-faced Aussies and sensed her fear. I doubted she could survive 70 days of heat, flies and clamoring crowds in Australia and New Zealand.

Then something wonderful happened. Her nanny handed Diana the infant Prince William. She was suddenly straight-backed and smiling, as if nothing could daunt her. From the day he was born, this child gave strength and purpose to an insecure young bride. Like any woman, she could look in the face of her first-born and realize she was a huge achiever; this perfect child eclipsed any failure or success in her life. If the Windsors made her feel trivial, she had William to remind them that, in less than a year of marriage, she had produced a future king. The obligatory Windsor Heir. Prince Harry–the Spare–only reinforced her triumph.

In the drama of Diana's funeral, it was easy for the bereaved world to overlook the personal tragedy of a mother's death. But we learned something important about William and Harry that day. They had inherited their mother's skill for silent statement and would insist the world knew their first priority. As the long coffin emerged from Kensington Palace, we saw an envelope propped against a wreath.

I believe the single word on the envelope was a press statement. By scrawling 'Mummy' large and loud, the boys were telling billions of people to forget the public property aspect of this incredible woman and remember what actually mattered to her. She was a mum. Few people knew that in their grief–and despite access to every florist in Europe–Diana's two boys had pushed each rosebud in the wreath themselves.

I often saw a younger William galloping to Diana after school. In his grubby hands he usually clutched some treasure made for mummy. When birthdays and Christmas came around, she always encouraged the boys to make her gifts. So the rosebud wreath was the boys' last present, showing mum they had not forgotten her values. Knowing how vital they were to her, William and Harry trudged after her coffin. They could not bear for mummy to make her final journey alone.

I once walked near Diana and toddler William in Kensington Park. A photographer got in their way and she said prettily: "I know it's your job to

OPPOSITE: One-year-old Prince William gets an early lesson in the art of the royal wave, Aberdeen, Scotland. TOP RIGHT: William is Diana's 'rock' during the grueling '83 Australian tour. BOTTOM: The Diana Memorial Garden in Kensington Park features a Peter Pan sailing ship and reflects the Princess' love for children.

Now with an heir, and a spare, to her credit, Diana is less daunted by in-laws on Buckingham Palace balcony. INSERT: New Zealand postage hails the birth of Prince Harry, '94. BOTTOM: Diana's pencil sketch of William reveals a mother's love and creditable artistry.

take pictures of me. I'm not cross. But remember, it's my job to be a mother." As the snow fell one winter in Cambridgeshire, roads closed and the Princess was late for a meeting of parents who had lost their babies to crib deaths. At last, she bounded in and I congratulated her on just getting through the snow. "Of course I had to come," she said. "I'm a mother, aren't I?"

Diana was creating a new mold for royal motherhood. Pregnancies were to be taken in her long stride, even if the first caught her unprepared. She found she could not zip her velvet Bruce Oldfield culottes and spent most of an Oxford St engagement with her hands clasped to her waist to stop the pants from descending. While I have never seen a picture of the Queen in a maternity dress, I saw a hugely increasing Diana climbing from helicopters and being swamped on strenuous walkabouts. Just a week before William arrived, I beheld her waddling around the Ascot races. Swathed in a taffeta tent, she danced with every man who had paid $200 to attend a charity event at Highgrove House. After multiple trips to the loo at Windsor polo grounds, she rolled her eyes and moaned: "Nobody told me about the morning sickness." Taking their cue from her frankness, the public was hardly compelled to be delicate. No sooner was William toddling than a Gloucester man asked her if she was again expecting. "You must be joking," she shot back. "I'm not on a production line."

All the same, her American friend Leona Shanks told me: "I think what she wanted more than anything in the world was a large family–and a happy marriage."

Indeed, at 19 years old Diana claimed, "I want lots and lots of children...I want to rival Queen Victoria." While not destined to be a brood mare along Victorian lines, motherhood was the making of Diana. Her confidence boomed when she realized those clamorous walkabouts–which earlier revealed her lack of conversation–were suddenly a pushover. In the past she had nothing to say to strangers. On becoming a mother, she was at last expert on something. Happily it was the subject closest to everyone's heart. I saw the change in Diana. While her husband shook hands and asked strangers "have you been waiting long to see me?" Diana assaulted waiting ears with the latest news on her baby. She talked about breast-feeding; about bath time. She said she slept with both her boys. She confided that William was especially fond of flushing his dad's hand-made shoes down the loo.

For the first time, the public received regular reports on a royal baby's progress - straight from the best authority. "I'm covered in drool, William's teething," she told me. "I'm having trouble sleeping. I have bags under my eyes," she regaled another mum. "I can't wait till William starts walking. Right now he's learning to spit...everyone thinks his nursery must be tidy. It's a terrible mess...he's a mini-tornado." She revealed her naughty boy's nickname. The Wombat. In more tender moments, the Princess confessed that William's skin was so scrumptious that she was tempted to "bite his botty." She astonished an Australian mum by declaring: "I wish I could change places with you and stay home all day with my baby." I pounced on this woman, who laughed: "Well, she's bloody nuts, isn't she?"

Banal as it all seemed, we reporters were over the moon. For the first time, those staple walkabouts were actually yielding copy. The public soon decided which of the Waleses was better value. When the Rolls Royce disgorged Diana on one side of the street and her husband approached the other side, a loud moan of "oh God, not *him*" was audible. He heard it, too. His ears, after all, are enormous.

It hardly made Charles love Diana more. But the public was enraptured. The masses warmed instantly to a person who was willing to share the most important thing in her life with strangers. Nor could children resist such warmth. "I warn you," she told a schoolboy who wanted to kiss her hand, "if you do you will never live it down." He did anyway. In Italy, an urchin escaped a police barricade to grab *Principessca Dee's* hand and toddle with the royal party for 10 minutes. In Alice Springs, Diana did a talk-show broadcast for Outback children. One little voice crackled over the wire, asking, "what is Prince William's favorite toy?" She grappled for political correctness and stammered: "He really loves his Australian koala bear." Then she rolled her eyes and added: "He has this whale that spouts things out the top. He has these little balls (blush)."

She wasn't perfect. A jealous mum, she had a habit of firing nannies who got too mummish and she was perfectly nasty to Tiggy Legge-Bourke, whom Charles hired to supervise the boys. Probably no child psychiatrist would approve Diana's tendency to involve schoolboy William as confessor, shrink and champion for all the troubled aspects of her life. The weight of the burden was obvious when William claimed he wanted to be a policeman when he grew up "so I can look after mummy." And yet, surrounded by courtiers who were paid to deceive her and report her every move, whom else could Diana trust? Even now, the grown up William is something of a policeman. Every new book that launches an attack on Diana's memory provokes an angry: "Leave my mother alone. She can't defend herself..."

Suffocating though mummy might have sometimes been, Diana had a down-to-earth hand in her sons' upbringing. I saw mother and boys queuing in McDonalds. At Christmas, they joined department store lines to see Santa Claus. They queued at amusement parks and waited for cinema tickets. When asked why she preferred high-street experiences for her boys, Diana insisted they would come to no harm in lines or traffic jams. She did not want them "going through life thinking everyone drove a Range Rover with all the lights magically turning green."

Said friend Leona Shanks: "She had her own ideas on raising the boys. She wanted them to have 'normal' childhood experiences. She knew the importance of what William was preparing for but (knew) without more normal experiences–which she thought would humanize him–he would be denied an understanding of ordinary people. She didn't want the boys kept

TOP: Diana created a new mold for royal working pregnancies and maternity fashions. On exhausting walkabouts, a billowing smock disguises her eight-month bulge. BELOW: William gets a reassuring pat from mummy on his first day at kindergarten school.

ABOVE: The most hands-on of royal mums, Diana was involved in every aspect of her sons' upbringing. Here she sprints in a parents' day race at Harry's Berkshire school. BELOW: Now that she's gone...numbed by mummy's sudden death, Diana's boys view bouquets outside Kensington Palace.

in an ivory tower. Even though she had been raised in privilege, she was in touch with reality."

When she thought the boys were ready, their mother showed them HIV hospices and homeless shelters. She was particularly proud when teenaged William helped entertain handicapped children who visited his prep school. It was a skill he inherited. At the same age, schoolgirl Diana had crawled on linoleum to make emotional contact with mental hospital patients. "A lot of adults couldn't handle that," she said of William's efforts. "Britain will be lucky to get William."

After visiting children's hospitals, Diana encouraged her sons to write get-well letters to sick children she had met. In a 1995 Panorama interview, she said: "I want them to have an understanding of people's emotions, people's insecurities, people's distress and people's hopes and dreams." She also said that if royalty were to remain relevant, the Windsors must learn to "walk hand in hand with the people." This sort of modernism made her in-laws cringe. But ironically, three years after Diana died, the Queen visited a McDonalds. The Monarch now wears gloves less often. Though the Windsors branded Diana a loose cannon they now reluctantly practice many of her populist ways.

ABOVE: On the funeral eve, Harry shows a brave face to mourners gathered outside Diana's London home. LEFT: Diana encouraged her sons to create presents like the gift a proud William (then five years old), took home from school. BELOW: A hand-made wreath on her coffin is the teenagers' farewell gift for 'Mummy.'

But I believe Diana's greatest legacy is her sons. Quite simply, the characters she helped form will determine the survival of the British Monarchy. William—so evidently Diana's son—has a good chance of keeping the Commonwealth as enraptured as his mother did. Having shared mummy's woes, He will surely shield his own wife from the chilly Windsors and the more rapacious media. For 16 years Diana tried to teach him the awesome responsibility in having the world's love. You must eternally give love back. No matter that your feet hurt, that your fingers are raw from handshaking, that your marriage is in tatters. Once I peered into the royal Rolls Royce and saw the world's most beloved woman, slumped in her Chanel suit, crying her eyes out. A minute later, Diana strode into the waiting crowd. Smiling, hand outstretched. She knew what people expected from Princess Diana.

Remember those pre-funeral newsreels of William and Harry, waist-high in flowers outside Kensington Palace? Having just lost the most important person in their lives, how could they face sympathetic onlookers? Heroically, stoically, they began clasping hand after hand, smiling and thanking strangers for their support. How did they do it? Mummy had shown them.

Boys to men. OPPOSITE: William, in his looks and manner so evidently Diana's son, may determine the survival of the British Monarchy. BELOW: The princes present clean-cut, hunky images in polo kit, Windsor, 2001.

CHAPTER FOUR
The Costumes

"Clothes make the woman. I know they certainly helped make me."
–DIANA'S WRITING, 1995.

Bruce Oldfield made Diana more than 60 outfits. I asked this designer how she managed to make any garment look fabulous. Was it her height (6ft in shoes)? Or her great shoulders? Her long legs? Her bosom? Oldfield pondered for a moment. "Her smile," he decided. "She was possessed of such radiance that dressed in a sack and under the weather, if she smiled, she dispelled the gloom."

Nevertheless, Diana's fashion image was based on a cutting-edge wardrobe, which we mortals eventually paralleled. I thought she had gone too far in a Galliano lingerie dress at the Metropolitan Museum in 1996. *Di wears her petticoat,* smirked the press. But when the lingerie-look swept chain stores three years later, I had a slip dress just like it. Thus was completed a full circle of Diana knock-offs. I had owned infinitely cheaper copies of her hats, frilly blouses, pearl chokers and sailor suits. Now, her petticoat.

But the melancholy truth is that Diana was in a fashion league of her own. As an ambassador for British fashion and bankrolled by her husband's millions, she owned more fabulous clothes than most people could imagine. Even Diana was appalled at the size of her wardrobe. It all started with the trousseau. "We had to go out and buy six of everything and we still didn't have enough," she said. "You have to change four times a day and suddenly, your wardrobe expands to something unbelievable."

By degrees, the Wales' palace apartments were redesigned around Diana's clothes. Most people will never see such a grand-scale wardrobe. But here is insight from artist Henry Mee, who sought a gown suitable for his 1995 portrait. He suggested a black evening dress. She offered 80ft of black models. "All the corridors had been partitioned and wardrobes put inside," he told me. "Each costume was so familiar, like looking at *Hello!* magazine photo shoots. She was in a difficult position, if she wore something she'd worn a lot, people accused her of not taking the occasion seriously. If she chose something new, she'd get criticized for that too." Eventually Mee chose a slim-fitting navy dress that did not dominate its wearer (See Chapter 6).

Leona, wife of American artist Nelson Shanks, witnessed a shyness about sartorial wealth. "We asked to see her wardrobe to select a dress. Most people are embarrassed because their clothes are in a mess. She was embarrassed because there were just so many. Each gown took up about a foot of space..."

Diana did not have a promising start in fashion. Aged 19, the kindergarten assistant wondered if she would be remembered for inspiring headlines like *the girl who forgot her petticoat.* At her first photo-call, she wore a cotton skirt and stood with the sun behind her. It certainly introduced Great Britain to the legs her stunned fiancé described as "spectacular."

**OPPOSITE: Diana in two-tone halter dress for the opera in '92. ABOVE: Adopting tartan as a sartorial statement, the Princess modernized Scotland's fashion image. In a Catherine Walker coatdress, she took plaid to Japan.
BELOW: Diana was posthumously awarded her own plaid. Designer Elizabeth Emanuel made this silk crinoline in Princess of Wales tartan.**

"Even among the supermodels," said designer Karl Lagerfeld, "there are no legs like this."

Pre-Charles, Diana had no sartorial vanity. Skirts, jeans and sweaters were her teenage uniform. For her first racetrack date with her royal beau, she borrowed a sister's coat and hat. "She was a typical English country girl," recalls Bruce Oldfield. "Brought up not to be too fussed about clothing. Of course, she soon got the bug. What started as a chore became a tool of her trade. When she first came to us at the beginning of the 80s, she had a bad stoop. I'd tell her to stand up straight. I had to be quite nannyish in keeping on at her. She was tall and she had quite a bosom. Later, she learned to capitalize on it."

Commentary on Diana's wardrobe began on the day of her engagement. All her career, any Wales' event was remembered by what the Princess wore. Some outfits were even given names, like the *Elvis*, the *Travolta*, or the *Grace Kelly*. As a crowd draw, her garments rated higher than Charles' sober speeches. The Queen Mother observed: "No one's going to show up to see (him) wearing the same suit, week after week." Neither would the fashion talk end, as Diana lay in her coffin in a new coatdress. She had progressed from the Margaret-Thatcherish suit that dominated her engagement pictures like an inkblot. Now she was a fashion legend.

But her haute couture debut got mixed reviews. Moslem nations banned pictures of her first official engagement, in the infamous black Emanuel crinoline. "It was a horrendous occasion," Diana recalled. The off-the-rack bodice delighted the tabloids by slipping down. "I was quite big-chested then," she said. "They all got frightfully excited." Realizing how out of her depth she was, the young bride recruited her fashion squad. Anna Harvey at Vogue filled an office with couturier clothes for Diana's inspection. The Bruce Oldfield Knightsbridge salon was an Aladdin's trove. The designer recalls those early Diana years: "The problem was, she'd been proclaimed the fount of British fashion. She had to wear clothes by British houses and she wanted to be democratic and support them all, irrespective of what suited her. She was catapulted into this 'glamour icon' scenario and it was hard for her; too many people were advising her on style. She went off in the fashion world like a kid in a candy shop. One day a big gown, the next a horrible, fussy hat."

Diana's hats evolved from a befeathered, veiled chapeau of '81 to confident millinery statements in the 90s. RIGHT: High-ho Silver! Diana aims to upstage actress Joan Collins in a Bruce Oldfield silver tissue model. By '85, the ingénue has moved to center-stage. "She loved being Diana," says Oldfield.

Fussy hats became de rigueur. In India, I saw Queen Elizabeth in a faithful copy of Diana's netted, beribboned boater. Though Her Majesty was not as fetching, she demonstrated that great or small, everyone copied the Windsor bride. If Diana's low heels sought not to dwarf her prince, *voila!* The world clumped around in flatties. But there were too many flounces; too many fancy necklines, polka dots–and her worst fashion crime–far too many bows. She hid behind fussy clothes. It was years before she overcame bulimia, built a more solid shape and exploited the unadorned column dress. (The bulimic years presented a problem for designers like Oldfield, who confided he "never knew whether to expect a thin or bigger Diana when she came for fittings. We often had to go back to square one and take her measurements again.")

In later years the Princess embraced a look that put her in the Jackie Kennedy league. No longer confined to British houses, she adopted the uncluttered sexiness of Versace and Chanel. But as Princess of Wales on tour, she had to sport British labels and took this duty seriously. Before any foreign tour, her mentors haunted Kensington Palace with ideas. "We'd sit on the floor," said Anna Harvey, "looking at sketches and fabrics. Once she called her husband into the drawing room to ask what he thought of a black Murray Arbeid dress. He just stared and said: 'You look absolutely wonderful!'"

Diana's true clothing genius was in matching her look to her situation. At the Cannes film festival, she wore the ice-blue chiffon, similar to Grace Kelly's *To Catch a Thief* model. She was so wonderful in Scottish plaid for the annual Braemar Games that she was posthumously awarded her own tartan. Lochcarron Of Scotland[1] now produces silks and woolens in the 'Princess of Wales' design–a blend of white and blue that also bears a Red Cross to echo Diana's patronage of that organization. She wore sailor hats to anything vaguely nautical. She used Pakistan's *shalwar kameez* outfits both in Moslem countries and at home. A Victor Edelstein ivory dress and bolero, worn to an Elysee Palace soiree with France's President Mitterrand, dripped lavish Napoleonic motifs. Knowing actress Joan Collins would be at a 1985 gala, the Princess had Oldfield run up the proto-type 'Dynasty-Di' showstopper in silver tissue. Its peek-a-boo back triggered gasps. "There were going to

1. To order Princess of Wales silk scarves or blankets, email: quality@Lochcarron.com

OPPOSITE: A Grace-Kelly inspired creation for the '95 Cannes Film Festival. **ABOVE LEFT:** Victor Edelstein used French imperial motifs to detail this ensemble for President Mitterand's Elysee Palace banquet. **RIGHT:** Embroidery on Catherine Walker's dress for India echoes both Mughal art and the Spencer tiara. **BELOW:** These three dresses were bought by the Romance Classic television network at the '97 Christie's charity auction.

be a lot of starry people there," the designer smiles fondly. "She wanted to be the shiniest. That was a good dress all around for her. She loved being center-stage. She loved being *Diana*." (There were more primitive gimmicks. At a ball in New Zealand, I saw the impish VIP tie a balloon to her priceless Queen Mary tiara. No one lost sight of her as she danced.)

Toward the end of her life, Diana discouraged the clotheshorse image. "I wish people would stop talking about my clothes," the humanitarian activist sighed. On her anti-landmine tours, she pointedly did not wash her hair and was seldom out of jeans. Mascara was her only makeup. When it suited, she proclaimed that the emphasis of media attention should not be on her clothing. But she never quite abandoned that flair for scene-stealing outfits. Separated from both her husband and the Royal Highness title, she snubbed convention and paraded femme-fatale gowns of unroyal black. Scooped backs presented a problem for gentlemen hosts. "They never know where to put their hands," she giggled. Hemlines ascended. At Roland Klein's salon, she commanded: "Shorter, shorter! Whatever I wear, I'll be criticized, so let's go for it."

Jacques Azagury said there was always a sexy aspect to Diana's designs. "I was never afraid to say, lower neckline; shorter skirt! She probably had the most fantastic legs in the world." According to the Princess' favorite design-

er, Catherine Walker, Diana's hemlines were "a barometer...to reflect her changing life. At the time of her divorce, they lengthened; shortly before her death they were probably shortest. I always liked (that) she didn't follow fashion but did what was right for her."

She knew her limits. "I would love a dress that's slashed to the waist," she told Oldfield. "But it isn't for me." There was no false modesty in fitting sessions; rather an impersonal model-girl professionalism. One male designer tried to exit while she changed. She cried: "No, stay!" He stared fixedly out across Kensington Park. Diana expected handsome discounts for clothing but unlike many celebrities, always paid her bills before they were due. Oldfield delighted in the flowers and thank-you notes she sent seamstresses. The fashion patron did not pinch pennies on her trademark frogging, sequins, exquisite lace and bugle beads. About 20,000 hand-stitched pearls weighed down Catherine Walker's famous *Elvis* outfit. Buttons on one cocktail dress were each worth $250.

As a divorcee, Diana had new reasons for dressing to kill. Sporting a

OPPOSITE: The famous "bathing suit" look, complete with wet hair, for the '92 New York Fashion Awards. **ABOVE:** A salute to the Rising Sun, in Tokyo. **ABOVE RIGHT:** A shoulder fan adds whimsy to this prim Emanuel dress for Bahrain. **RIGHT:** The limbs couturier Jacques Azagury called "the most fantastic legs in the world."

According to designer Bruce Oldfield, Diana's smile was her greatest asset. "Dressed in a sack and under the weather (her smile) dispelled the gloom," he says. Here a boned Valentino neckline frames the perfect smile.

ABOVE: An enviable bosom is a superb form for this navy column dress, worn to a '97 film premiere. RIGHT: Diana is both flamboyant and tailored in a fuchsia Catherine Walker ensemble at the Windsor Garter Ceremony. Gloves were a rarity; she wore them only as fashion accessories.

wisp of black chiffon, she could trump Charles for press attention and invite unflattering comparisons of a frumpy mistress and gorgeous, betrayed wife. Diana's ego loved the buzz of being the most famous, most glamorous star at any event. But remember, glamour was her most powerful fund-raising tool. Says Oldfield: "She committed herself to looking good because it was a way of doing her job well." Catherine Walker defends Diana's dressing to titillate journalists. "The press became her mirror. So what if she was a little vain? If she hadn't been, she would never have become the person we (loved) so." One outfit never mirrored by the press was Walker's last commission for her patron; a dress to be buried in. "A little part of me will be with her forever," says the designer.

Four years after the funeral, I drove over the Sierra Nevada into Ponderosa country, seeking a satin relic of the Princess. Maybe it was not a mission for someone whose interest in the lady was always professional. But now, I believe my career spent trailing in Diana's size-nine footsteps was an experience to turn a hack into an historian. Well, a pop historian. But pop is relevant and if a dress—which a divorced princess fancied as a wedding gown—hung in a Nevada vault, I wanted to see it. In 200 years, I reasoned, Diana's lace would be as historical as Napoleon Bonaparte's old breeches.

The 15-year-old Bruce Oldfield model was in good shape. Its satin slithered eagerly from a calico bag. The cool yardage tumbled through my gloves and stretched almost as tall as its former owner. I recalled the young Cinderella I watched fleeing a hundred formal banquets; how wry she had been about those gilded cage metaphors. She once joshed a chum of mine—who was leaving Kensington Palace to visit Wormwood Scrubs Prison—"ha, you're going from one prison to another!"

Selling that Oldfield and 78 other gowns in 1997 was a casting off of

ABOVE: Passionate about eastern culture in her last years, she wears a pearl-studded *shalwar kameez* for an outing with Pakistani friend Imran Khan.

shackles for Diana. They were part of a life as choking as her marriage. At Prince William's suggestion, she used the Christie's auction to raise $3.2 million for charity. Three months later, she was rid of all restraints. Forever. Like the face that stays eternally 36 years old while the rest of us age, the dress hung–frozen in a time warp–from my fingers. It was easy to imagine her shoulders peeking through the lace. A wealthy Tahoe woman had paid $29,000 for the model at the New York auction. (Christie's dresses sold for eight times the auction price after Diana's death.) The Nevada owner, whom I call Nancy, is no princess fanatic. Like many Americans, she respects a survivor's resilience. "She was a great example to modern women," Nancy told me. "If Diana had a problem, she dealt with it. She always held her head high."

"At the sale, the auctioneer banged his gavel like he wanted me to have that dress. I would have bought another, but I wasn't quick enough." The real thrill was meeting Diana at the auction preview party. The Princess quizzed Nancy: "You're here to buy one of my dresses? Which one?" Next day, Nancy set her sights on the demure white Oldfield because Diana had identified it as the one dress "that could be used for a wedding gown." A romantic endorsement, even if she had only worn it for an art exhibition and a private banquet.

Designer Oldfield remembers his client pirouetting in the ivory satin at the final fitting. Now Nancy keeps it in a vault. As I helped repack the relic, I saw that the hemline that floated joyfully around a princess' dancing feet was now sadly rumpled. After years in Kensington Palace's perfumed closets, Cinderella's dress was sentenced to a Tahoe vault.

As its first owner had said, "from one prison to another..."

Girl talk. Observing Moslem protocol at an
Oman university, Diana retreats to the
women's corner with female students.

CHAPTER FIVE
The Road Show

"Eat your heart out, Brazil!"

—DIANA, APPROVING DRESS DESIGNS FOR
HER SOUTH AMERICAN TOUR, 1996

It was eve of Charles and Diana's New Zealand tour–the second Commonwealth outpost the Waleses visited together–and I chatted to Diana over cocktails. Taking a native's liberty, I alluded to tribal customs. "You'll have to press noses for the *hongi* greeting," I said. She fingered her noble Norman proboscis. "I'm not sure about my aim...I hope I won't hurt anyone." I suggested she practice on her husband. "I don't want to give him such a thrill," she giggled. When I promised she would be transported in a war canoe paddled by more than100 half-naked warriors, she feigned nonchalance: "Sounds exactly like the Queen's yacht."

In the event, Diana's cultural experience of this (and any) country was plain sailing. Lady Beattie, wife of the late New Zealand Governor General, told me "she had no proper mentor to show her the way, she was pitched in the deep end and did extremely well. Nothing fazed her." Indeed, she encountered customs more exotic than chanting warriors. The Princess danced with a disco idol in the USA. She was kimono wrapped, sushi-style in Japan. Her forehead was daubed in India. The English Rose tripped across scattered rose petals in Pakistan. She covered her hair in mosques and was veiled in black for the Vatican. No princess of Wales grasped so many hands in as many countries as Diana. After long days of Australian walkabouts, the royal visitors soothed crushed fingers in iced water.

And no princess of Wales was so internationally adored, even in countries where royalty had been given the boot. *"Principessca Dee!"* the Romans screamed. Finicky Frenchmen complimented her English clothes. After her visit to Versailles, designer Pierre Cardin simpered: "This is the home of the Sun King of France, now we have a Sun Princess of Versailles." I noticed American flags during a Canadian walkabout. Thousands of New Yorkers had driven across the border to see Diana. "She's our princess, too," insisted the day-trippers.

They would have their chance the following year, when even celebrities in the White House gawped like children at the star in their midst.

A compulsive mimic, Diana nailed the East Coast dialect and convulsed herself with nasal New York tributes: "Hey, howyuh doin Di?" or "don'yuh juss lawk goyjuss!" In fact, she loved America. Her Philadelphian friend Leona Shanks explained Diana's affection for the place. "In Britain she was under a microscope. America did

TOP RIGHT: Lady in red. A contemporary legend strides into Eva Peron's Buenos Aires. BOTTOM RIGHT: Happy to nose you. Diana adopts local tradition to press noses in the *hongi*, a New Zealand Maori greeting.

Ola! A vivid satin tuxedo and bow tie
delight Lisbon, where Diana attended an
'87 gala ballet performance.

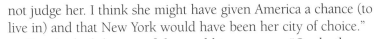

not judge her. I think she might have given America a chance (to live in) and that New York would have been her city of choice."

But she had the rest of the world to conquer. "Oooh, those eyes," moaned nuggety Australian Prime Minister Bob Hawke. Portuguese President Mario Soares became a blushing mess when, in view of Lisbon officials, Diana twanged his trouser braces. French President Giscard d'Estaing wrote: "When (she) spoke, she lifted her eyes towards me, those immense blue eyes. That's when I discovered she was also a cat, a feline. She moves without noise..." A Canadian politician botched his banquet speech and admitted intoxication: "I was drunk on her charm." She could even win hearts with an insult. "You are a pest," she snapped at a Nova Scotia photographer. "The next time I see a camera so close I'll kick it!" Drooled the shutterbug: "Oh, she's great..." On the same visit, I asked a garage mechanic to rate the royal handshake. "I can't talk," he stammered. "I can't describe how I feel. I touched her."

Always the ballet dancer, Diana stepped daintily through protocol. Shoeless when custom demanded. Though probably more fascinating to Eastern rulers than her husband–they heaped her with an emir's ransom in jewels–she accepted female exclusion from royal gatherings. The politics of fashion was her forte. She delighted in echoing local customs with her clothes and jewels. Donning the colors of their flags, she wordlessly saluted host nations. Her dress was dotted with rising suns in Tokyo. I noted her best visual coup in Edmonton, where the jagged collar of her Vanvelden under-blouse fell like a maple leaf across a red suit. Oh Canada!

Quite often though, it was what Diana did *not* wear that showed her cultural sensitivity. Planning a trip to Brazil, she avoided blue, green and yellow (colors of the Brazilian footballers who had just lost the World Cup to Argentina). More importantly, said her couturier Catherine Walker, the royal

TOP: Princess of whalebones. Victorian garb for a barbecue in Edmonton, Canada.
CENTER: A rose from a British parachutist surprises regimental chief Diana in Berlin.
RIGHT: pajamas and finger food for a desert picnic in Saudi Arabia.

VIP could not sport the blue and white soccer colors of Argentina. "This would have caused a riot."

At the time of her marriage breakdown, she hankered to become a roving ambassador for Britain. She certainly had the courage. In Pakistan, her hairdresser Sam McKnight stumbled tearfully behind Diana during grim walkabouts among the diseased. Only to watch his boss, kneeling, touching and being touched.

If the Palace thought that the young consort's first overseas tour would ease Diana into her role, they reckoned without the salivating Australians and New Zealanders. This meet-the-Princess campaign turned out to be the longest, most difficult and most important trip for the young mother. She thought bringing baby William would ease things. In fact, it increased the strain. The press party dubbed the 70-day circus the 'baby tour'. No matter where the parents stopped on the vast Australian continent, they returned to William's New South Wales billet every night, covering thousands of extra miles and exhausting everyone. For most of the visit Diana was homesick and dead-tired. Though terrified of doing wrong, she aced everything by simply being herself. She talked non-stop about her baby and was showered with praise and kisses. "Why don't you kiss my husband," she teased a woman. (Remember by contrast, the absurd fuss when an African American matron hugged the Queen in Washington DC?) Diana accepted all embraces. She remembered: "It was make or break time for me. I learned how to be 'royal' in one week. The whole world was focusing on me every day." Of the Sydney madhouse, she marveled: "My husband had never seen crowds like that and I sure as hell hadn't!"

Diana made no speeches in Australia, but everyone adored her little radio broadcast to Outback children. Her clipped accent and blushes contrasted with the youngsters' boldness, but she tried not to sound prissy.

"Has Prince William got a bicycle?"

"Um, no...he's a bit small" (he was eight months old).

"How many teeth has Prince William got?"

"He's got six teeth so the next big thing is his starting to crawl."

By New Zealand, he had taken that baby step. The red knees of rug-rat burn announced his achievement and the crowning event of the entire tour was the first royal crawlabout. Princely in silk rompers, the Wombat was plonked down for his first command performance. We waited breathlessly. Would he or wouldn't he? Aaah, he would. Dutifully William lurched toward his wooden Buzzy Bee toy. After entertaining generations of Kiwi children, the humble bumble now had the next best thing to a royal warrant.[1]

TOP: Baby William delights his parents during the first royal crawlabout in New Zealand.
FAR RIGHT: A stamp iconizes a toy beloved of princes and generations of Kiwis.
ABOVE: Diana dons exotic colors of Asia for her '87 Thailand visit.

1. Buzzy Bee website: www.buzzybee.co.nz.

In the much-anticipated *hongi,* a Maori schoolgirl was the first to press noses with Diana. Hearing of Diana's death 15 years later, she recalled the pallor and softness of the Princess' skin and how, in her nervousness, she squashed the royal foot. "She was a nice lady and very beautiful. To think, I *hongied* her..."

Sir David and Lady Beattie loaned their Auckland mansion to the Waleses family as a home base. "William had crawled days before, in Australia," Lady Beattie said. "But they saved the announcement and the picture opportunity for New Zealand. I think they thought it would be something special for us. He was such a smiley baby and Diana said, 'here, have a go!' and handed him to (Sir) David and me to hold. His legs were lovely and dimpled and he really looked at your face. Diana treated our house as their own. She came downstairs in her dressing gown and played the piano–classical things. Her nanny and a policeman went off every day like a married couple and took Prince William to the beach or shopping. No one ever recognized him. Charles and Diana were envious that they could never do that."

British newspapers kept the Waleses abreast of their home press. Diana was not always pleased with what she read. "They tried to stop her from reading certain stories," said Lady Beattie. "She insisted and she was upset when things weren't reported as she wanted. It was stressful for her." There was also a growing domestic tension. Tactless in their preference for Diana, colonials left the Prince of Wales baffled and hurt. "It would have been far easier to have two wives to cover both sides of the street," he told an Auckland banquet. "I could have walked down the middle directing the operation." Guests tittered but I saw Diana wilt. Her popularity no longer delighted her husband. As Canadian masses screamed for Diana later that year, her prince muttered: "I'm only here to collect flowers."

Her fans were more gallant. In Spain, students laid down their cloaks Walter Raleigh-style, for her to walk on. A British soldier in Germany parachuted from the sky and gave the astonished visitor a red rose. The Sultan of Oman parted with a fortune in diamonds and sapphires. A besotted Pierre Trudeau praised "this radiant lady with the beautiful eyes." Among Canadians, Diana-smooching became so epidemic that an official no-kissing rule had to be issued. When critics called her clothes old fashioned, she showed them old fashioned. She aired an authentic Edwardian costume (borrowed from the BBC wardrobe) for a Gay 90s barbecue at Edmonton. This was a magical scene. Diana's long stride was slowed by her button boots, bustle and boning. I felt she had just stepped off a chocolate box lid. Shattering the illusion, she later told me, "I was so glad to get out of that dress. It was whalebone throat to waist."

ABOVE LEFT: Dueling bonnets. The Princess meets her millinery match in Canada.
ABOVE: With white puritan collar and red suit, Diana wordlessly salutes the Canadian maple leaf flag.
BELOW: Obeying religious protocol, Diana ditches Chanel pumps and covers her hair for a mosque visit in Pakistan.

BELOW: Tea in the White House with
First Lady Nancy Reagan is followed
by toast with the President.
OPPOSITE: Diana trips the light
fantastic with the Gipper and
BELOW: Jitterbugs with disco idol
John Travolta.

Photos, Ronald Reagan Library.

By the time they hit Italy in 1985, *Diana e Carlo* had two sons. But William and Harry were not *bambini* enough for the natives or the local newspapers. Headlines claimed that Diana wanted *a baby from Charles made in Italy*. Gossips said that the royal yacht's chef served pasta with aphrodisiac sauce. Less endearing for Diana was the daily carping criticism of her clothes. Italian writers were incensed that she did not bring an entirely new wardrobe; they were outraged when she graced La Scala in an "ugly and banal dress more suited to a shop assistant." And she had worn it *twice* before! Romans offered no laurels. Comics yelled "waiter!" at her white suit and black bow tie. Couturiers were not always to blame. Her linguini-thin, bulimic shape did nothing for their designs.

But Victor Edelstein's velvet White House dress knocked the socks off a celebrity crowd. An admiring and flustered President Reagan introduced his guest as "Princess David." In a moment of glory, Diana signed Mikhail Baryshnikov's place card and told the ballet dancer how she once waited in the rain at Covent Garden for his autograph. First Lady Nancy Reagan told John Travolta that the guest of honor secretly wanted to dance with him. "Of course, as soon as they started dancing, everyone stood aside and watched with awe," she said. "It was just the two of them and they were beautiful to behold." Travolta told me: "For 15 lovely minutes, she made me feel like a prince. It was magical..." Charles was less princely as reporters rehashed the Travolta tableau in lieu of recording his speeches. "My wife would be an idiot if she didn't enjoy dancing with John Travolta," he snapped.

The prospect of dancing with Diana became the main attraction for any American fundraiser. General Colin Powell stood up with the regal divorcee at a 1996 gala. As they foxtrotted, he crooned: *"Heaven, I'm in heaven."* He rejoiced later: "I'm a nifty dancer. But not as nifty as she is!" Designer Calvin Klein also had the honor and shared an animated conversation with his dance

It's a wrap. Hosts of the '86 Japan tour present a kimono and insist on an immediate costume change for a giggling Diana.

partner. The topic? "We were discussing my underwear," Klein said. "She wears it."

In countries where women have less status, Diana stayed out of the spotlight. For a 1986 tour of the Gulf States, her fashions bared little more than ankles, hands and face. But Saudi royalty romanced her with a desert picnic straight out of a Valentino movie. Bedouin tents, priceless carpets, sand dunes and white stallions were the props. Effortlessly chic in silk pajamas, Diana sat cross-legged and ate with her fingers.

At best, Charles and Diana's tours were a boon for diplomacy, trade and British fashion. At worst, press reports chronicled a disintegrating marriage. In the Portuguese sojourn of 1987, we learned the couple sought separate hotel suites. By Korea, 1992, their suites were on different floors. Diana used stunning props to upstage or snub Charles. In the flight up Ayers Rock, she left her husband in her red dust. When she mooched alone by the romantic Sphinx, the world ached for her isolation. The Wales' road show was scrapped after their final, dismal tour of Korea. By then, we had given up on romantic headlines and labeled them *The Glums*, after a doleful British radio family.

Divorce was their next destination. Ten years as joint ambassadors for Britain were history. "We would have made the best team in the world," Diana said. "I could shake hands till the cows come home. And Charles could have made serious speeches. But it was not to be." Still, those 10 years defined the ingénue's poise. Once I saw a 20-year-old princess weeping on the deck of her honeymoon yacht, overcome by crowds singing her off to sea. Years later, I had goose bumps during her jeep ride among 62,000 Canadians who lustily sang *"Happy birthday dear Diana."* She seemed pleased but not overwhelmed. She had seen it all before.

The world her classroom, Diana had graduated *summa cum laude.*

TOP: Brilliant costumes of Cameroon ladies overshadow the visitor's sober designer attire. BOTTOM: The Wales take a jeep ride as 62,000 Canadians pack a stadium to sing "Happy birthday dear Diana."

CHAPTER SIX

The Publicity Stills

"Peace is breaking out..."
—DIANA, WRITING TO FRIEND
LEONA SHANKS, 1996

During 50 sittings for a '94 portrait, American Nelson Shanks and his wife Leona befriend the royal model. BELOW: self-portrait by Shanks. OPPOSITE: "An exquisite, sensitive soul," as seen by the artist. The canvas now adorns Althorp, the Spencer ancestral home in Northamptonshire.

By the summer of 1994, what the Archbishop of Canterbury had called "the stuff of fairytales" was exposed as a myth. Embarrassing stories about Diana's private life and alleged nuisance phone calls to antique dealer Oliver Hoare–compounded by Charles' admission of his adultery–saw the Princess at her most vulnerable. But for this consummate professional, life went on. She sat for her second-to-last painted portrait. The wistful study by American Nelson Shanks captured more than her elegance. It freeze-framed a disillusioned but stoic refugee. "I meant to chronicle a time in history and an exquisite, sensitive soul and what it was enduring," the painter told me. "Also, what there was in her character that would see her through."

The Princess hung the canvas at Kensington Palace. It now adorns the family gallery at Althorp. As much for Shanks' friendship as his genius, the painting was Diana's favorite image of herself.

Because her emerald 'skirt' had to stay draped on a mannequin, Diana posed in her blouse and slip. "She was not at all shy," says Shanks of his model. "She was mature and professional." *Photo, Leona Shanks.*

In 50 hours of private sittings, Diana, Shanks and his wife Leona developed a camaraderie that supported the Princess through the heartbreaking dissolution of her marriage. It also gave the Shankses a rare understanding of the forces driving their friend. Astonished at her isolation and eagerness for diversion, they took Diana to restaurants and galleries. They protected her in ugly paparazzi encounters. They entertained her in New York and stayed in touch. As Americans, they were not cowered by royalty. As a long-time painter of the famous, Shanks was unfazed by her celebrity. "If I had put on airs or been overcome by her, it would not have worked. We hit it off on a basic level and worked well together. I adored her. It was a painful, hurtful time for Diana. At every turn, somebody was accusing her of something. She was getting astonishingly little support and I thought we were her only champions. Many times I felt like I just wanted to wrap her up and take her somewhere safe. Charles had just done that TV interview in which he'd admitted his adultery but failed to mention that he'd ever loved her. I think she was more hurt by this omission than by anything he *did* say. At this stage–even up to a year later–she would have taken him back in a heartbeat. She remained in love with him, or with an idea of him. It took her a long time to realize it was over, over, over..."

Shanks' portrait of a lady began in Kensington Palace. "Leona and I waited in the drawing room, surrounded by some of the Queen's great paintings. I expected a demure princess but suddenly there was this thundering of feet through the house. It was Diana. So alive and athletic. I bowed and Leona curtseyed as best she could and Diana seemed surprised. Leona called her Your Highness and she said: "Let's get this straight. We are going to be friends and you are going to call me Diana." The painter described his Chelsea studio. "Let's do the sittings at your place," she decided. "I want to get out of here."

The first task was choosing a dress for the portrait. Diana was reluctant to show her wardrobe. She said: "I'm sorry, it's so big..." Shanks recalled "an embarrassment of riches. A succession of (shudder) prom dresses, one after another. All in pastels, I don't like painting that sort of thing. We chose a low-cut thing. I was doing my first sketch and I knew I did not want it. It looked like a cocktail dress. The image was shallow, not lasting. I said I was interested in a white blouse. She didn't have one but by the next day they'd got 20 of them together at Kensington Palace. She put on this Starzewski one and she looked out of this universe. It was more than just a blouse. In it, she was ethereal. She glowed..."

"She had a beautiful neck. I asked if she had a choker. She said: 'Would Queen Mary's emeralds do?' We broke out laughing. They were huge. I'm sure they were worth trillions and she insisted on leaving them in the studio overnight–a nightmare for me–I had to convince her not to." For the skirt, couturier Catherine Walker draped some green taffeta on a mannequin. Diana did all her sittings in the Starzewski blouse and her petticoat. "She was not at all shy," approved Shanks. "She was mature and professional."

Once a bond had formed between Diana and the Shankses, her loneliness was exposed. They were astonished by how eager she was for any outing. "I expected her to plead a busy schedule. But it was like the engine was running and she was ready to go. I think she was anxious to get out in the world no one would take her. She was not judgmental; she was available for anything. If I said let's go to the Royal Academy exhibition or let's go to dinner, she'd say, 'yes!' I think that's probably what happened with this Dodi thing–he asked her to the South of France and she probably just said, 'yes!' It was beyond my imagination that someone with her incredible personality should not have had more options available, that this exquisite creature did not have a man. People thought she was unapproachable, unavailable..."

ABOVE: Trembling British upper lip. As she faces the end of her marriage and humiliating rumors about her private life, Diana's moods swing between laughter and tears. "She often arrived at the studio crying," recalls Leona Shanks. BELOW: The Shankses introduced Diana to Luciano Pavarotti. In turn, Pavarotti introduced Diana to dining *en famille*.

RIGHT: Girl next to the door. Bryan Organ, 1981. Fiancée Diana Spencer is isolated at Buckingham Palace, waiting for her prince to come home from a Commonwealth tour. In her first official portrait, the teenager seems daunted by her surroundings. Her garments conceal her figure. Reacting to being called "chubby" by Charles, she has begun her bulimia habit. *Picture, National Portrait Gallery, London.*

The media was abuzz with the infamous doings in the House of Wales. Braving mobs of press, Diana often arrived at the studio in tears. "I don't think it was entirely what was happening in the marriage," said Shanks. "Lots of her pain was because of public opinion of her. I knew it was a time she needed to do a lot of talking and how often did she get this kind of opportunity?" Leona Shanks told me: "She'd be sitting, posing, and suddenly you'd see she'd been thinking of something painful. Her face flushed and tears welled up in her eyes. Twenty minutes later, she'd be laughing."

On a whim, the painter invited Diana to the opening of a Venetian exhibition at the Royal Academy. "I found I was in hot water. I had previously tried to get a ticket for lord so-and-so and was told no, not another person could come. Leona phoned the academy and said we *must* bring the Princess of Wales. By the time we got there the next day, there was a reception line for her. She had often apologized for her lack of formal education. I think her secretary, Patrick Jephson, was kind of stuffy, preppy and liked to play against her. But I took her around the exhibition and I remember how astute her remarks were, like she'd had a good, basic art education." A thank-you note in Diana's big, generous hand followed any outing.

The Three Dianas. John Merton, 1985. The Wiltshire portraitist preferred serious poses to Diana's usual smiling image. "She was very happy and amusing," Merton says. "My wife was talking and (Diana) asked if she could talk back. I said yes, as long as she shut her mouth occasionally. She said: 'Nobody ever said that to me.' Her detective came in to see her portraits and he looked at a large, triple nude. She said: 'No, not that picture!'" *Picture, courtesy John Merton.*

Cropped hair and cropped out of a marriage. Douglas Anderson, 1991. Diana's 30th birthday and 10-year wedding anniversary have passed, uncelebrated. The artist paints rigid hands, clenched jaw and a stiff upper lip. Anderson's wife told me: "People asked why he painted her so sad. She was sad. It was absolutely the worst time for her." *Picture, courtesy Douglas Anderson.*

Still the ingénue. June Mendoza, 1983. Just before her second pregnancy, Diana is rail-thin and stooped. Anorexia rumors are rampant. "I painted her with that slightly shy look," June Mendoza remembers. "She changed her posture later, as she became more grown up. She was a dear, thoughtful girl. When I returned to the palace just to paint the background, she always left a little bouquet and a note. She didn't have to do that." Picture, courtesy June Mendoza.

"The envelopes were on the doormat the next morning. Her father had always insisted she should not let any time pass before sending thank-you notes. In restaurants she would offer her credit card and try to pay. She'd say: 'It's all right Nelson, Charles owes me a lunch.' I never let her pay. I'm old-fashioned."

He found Diana funny and self-deprecating. "One night I admired her Chanel shoes. She pointed out the double-C logo and said: 'I call these my Charles and Camilla shoes.'

"I was painting Margaret Thatcher the same summer. (Baroness Thatcher) had left a photograph of herself, signed 'all the best, Margaret Thatcher.' Diana saw it. Next day, she brought a much bigger color portrait in a silver frame. Tiara and all. It was signed 'to Nelson and Leona, with *much* love.' I guess she wanted to love us more and be loved more...I made one blunder, she was trying to help me professionally and she asked if there was anyone in England I'd like to paint? I said 'yes, Prince Charles'–I mean, he has these large ears and bright blue eyes and he'd be great to paint–but there was an awful silence from Diana. She didn't find that funny."

ABOVE: Althorp's Lady of the Lake, complete with island, temple and roses. A prophetic vision by David Hankinson, 1992. *Picture, courtesy David Hankinson.*

Diana met tenor Luciano Pavarotti through the Shankses. "She was in New York and I arranged dinner with Luciano at the National Arts Club. We were going to pick her up in Luciano's tacky white stretch limousine but the British Consulate said no. They would get her there. So they closed off Lexington and Park Avenue. Consequently, we were blocked and arrived 45 minutes late. I had stood Princess Diana up! For dinner, she had shrimp in sauce. Luciano eyed her plate and asked if he could taste it. She nervously agreed and he started eating off her plate, quite undaunted. And then he passed it to his girlfriend. Diana told me, quietly: 'I'm not used to this...'"

After the painting was complete, Diana wrote regularly to Leona. In 1996, following the divorce, she wrote: "Peace is breaking out." Said Leona: "I think it was really the calm before the storm." One week before the accident that ended Diana and Dodi Fayed's lives, Nelson Shanks woke suddenly in New York, crying: "Diana, this is not a good idea!" The same warning haunted him all next day. "I am not a believer in psychic stuff," he said. "But she was due back in London on the Sunday. I would give her a day with her sons then call her and tell her she needed to be *here*; we needed to protect her.

"The accident was on Saturday night in Paris. A friend phoned and said Diana had broken her arm. I imagined her in a cast. Three hours later, I heard she was dead. It was like a bomb going off in my chest..."

ABOVE: Shades of Dorian Gray. Henry Mee, 1995. Diana's image is painfully bruised, as if emerging from a fractured past. The divorce is under way and she is raw about her treatment. It is the last official portrait of Diana. "People didn't know what she really looked like," says Mee. The media kept this image of a 19-year-old. But she was older, more mature. You could see what she'd been through; she was a very strong woman. She'd left all that Lady Di stuff behind." The model's opinion of the Mee study? "It's great. I love it!" *Picture, courtesy Henry Mee.*

LEFT: A preliminary facial study by David Hankinson reveals Diana's effect on the artist. "I fell in love with her," he said. "Because of the remarkable warmth she exuded...she had a magic." Behind Diana's apparent serenity, Hankinson sees troubled eyes. "The stress was something I felt in the short period I knew her. Stress, stress, stress."

Here's looking at you. A sidelong glance spots a camera. Diana claimed she could sense a photographer 100 yards away. **OPPOSITE:** Baptism by fire. Flashlights illuminate the dazed teenager on her first night out as a fiancée.

CHAPTER SEVEN
The Press Notices

"I'm a product that sells well."

—DIANA, IN A 1993 INTERVIEW.

In 1994, Diana's American friends Nelson and Leona Shanks took the Princess to dinner in London. Nelson later told me about the experience. "The public in the restaurant was nice—nobody stared—it was a lovely evening until we came to leave. We stepped out into the dark and bang! Two paparazzi[1] in black leather were in her face, snapping. Her little green car was a block away and they walked backwards in front of her. I was holding her hand, trying to get between them. She almost couldn't open her car door but when she did, one photographer threw himself on the bonnet, still snapping through the windshield. She was crying. Next day, the newspapers headlines said *Princess in tears*. Like she was some psycho going around London weeping. They didn't say they had made her cry. Till then, it had been a wonderful evening..."

By the 90s, such was Diana's life. Yet it had not always been that way. When it was feared that Diana was beleaguered by press attention in the first year of her marriage, the Queen invited newspaper editors for drinks and politely asked them to call off the news hounds. They did. When I first joined the Palace team, the press approach to the Windsors was as genteel as cricket. We read the Court Circular and showed up at royal engagements on our best behaviour. I remember Prince Charles approaching a cluster of his press entourage, to kindly ask: "Are you all getting enough to eat and drink?" Always a major concern for news people! As I watched Prince Philip driving his carriage at the Windsor Horse Trials, I talked casually to a comfy British matron beside me. Only when I looked in her face did I realize I had been chatting up the Queen. Her detectives did not deem me a threat and she seemed unperturbed.

Photographers kept a respectful distance from her young daughter-in-law. When Diana was photographed in a bikini—while expecting William—the audacity of this invasion was bigger news than the photo itself and the offending newspaper was obliged to apologize to the Queen, Diana and to its outraged readers. All this was about to change. In the summer of 1982, French picture agencies shrugged at the namby-pamby British press. They had made a fortune for years by snapping the unguarded moments of Monaco's Princess Caroline and Greek heiress Christina Onassis. When this philosophy arrived in England, it quickly changed the nature of celebrity. We had recorded royals if they did newsworthy things; foreign agencies found it newsworthy enough that Grimaldis, Onassises and now Diana, simply breathed. Thus celebrating celebrity for celebrity's sake seeped into

---

1. Paparazzi originated in Italy. These freelance photographers filled newspapers with 'stolen' images and were the bane of celebrities' lives. Princess Grace's '56 Monaco wedding heralded a paparazzi hey-day that continued unimpeded until Princess Diana's death-chase in 1997.

Like Alice...once a princess steps through the looking glass lens and beckons the press into her private life, there is no turning back.

the unwary British media's habits and quickly took hold. French agencies correctly pronounced Diana an untapped fortune. In 1982, a paparazzo came to London and moved into an hotel beside my flat. I lunched with him most days; amused by his outrageous stories. He parked outside Kensington Palace every morning. Wherever Diana went, he followed and sent snaps to Paris. Before long, British papers resented his scoops. They commissioned London freelancers to imitate the Frenchman. He was a hard act to follow. Unlike the rest of us, he had no conscience about peeving the Royals. Returning from trespassing on Sandringham Estate, he showed me photos of Diana glumly riding beside the Queen. As he was snapping the startled and unprotected women, the Queen had coldly pronounced: "Young man, you are very rude." Censure from my monarch would have crushed me. The Frenchman laughed fit to bust!

Diana became (and let herself become) the focus of not just a global industry, but of human fantasy. Through her, consumers found a dream that blended an old fairytale with the modern elixir of super-celebrity. She was everything we could not be. Universally loved, absurdly beautiful, rich, thin and more famous than anyone alive. In her triumphs, she was a heroine. In her failures, a martyr. In her follies, she garnered compassion. In decrying the Windsors for not mourning Diana's death sufficiently, both public and press felt less guilty for their part in loving this woman to death. Mario Testino, Diana's friend and personal photographer, considered her loss a hard cultural lesson. "We are all implicated in the invasion (of Diana's privacy)," he said after the funeral. "It comes from a desire to have more and more of something we crave...that wonderful smile and the allure she possessed. All of us demanded this invasion."

It is pointless to argue whether the press created or simply fed an addiction to Diana. She sold tabloids faster than Martian landings. "I'm a product that sells well," she realized. Experts say that if Diana had not become a princess, she might have run the most successful PR business on earth. The true mark of her skill was that, at her death, many considered her a victim and not a media creation. In her 1995 BBC interview, Diana shrugged: "There were three of us in this marriage, so it was a bit crowded." But Camilla Parker Bowles was just part of the jam. From the earliest days, Diana welcomed a fourth wheel into the Wales household. Charles might never have proposed had not Diana–while her prince dithered–seduced the press. Head down in the streets of Earls Court, she was able to look both shy and photogenic. The Windsors approved her decorum. But the silent star managed to convey her message with smirks and blushes. Charles was in doubt; Fleet St was in love. "I expect it will be the right thing in the end," Charles sighed and popped the massive sapphire on Diana's finger. She had enlisted the media to make her a princess. On a summer day in 1981, her allies took position–cameras trained like shotguns–for The Wedding.

War makes for strange bedfellows. When the Royal Family grew jealous and critical of the new girl's ways, Diana relied on pictures and headlines to underscore her success. The Windsors were easy to upstage. A new hairstyle or polka-dot socks did the trick. She could not make her husband love her but public adulation eased the hole in her heart. Princess Anne sniffed that Diana "obviously filled a void in the media's life which I had not filled."

If her in-laws had thought Diana would simply breed chins and height into the next generation, they were pathetically late in acknowledging her real gift. Even I sniggered when the Queen's press secretary told me, in 1981, that his boss expected Diana-fever to abate "a year or so after the wedding." Greater foresight had come from Princess Grace, who told Diana,

Charles might never have proposed had not Diana seduced the press with her photogenic silent-star vulnerability. The canny 19-year-old enlisted the media to make her a princess.

Postcards from the edge, '92. Diana con-
trives images to show how ill used she is in
her marriage. The world's most adored
woman is achingly alone at the Taj Mahal,
the Sphinx and the Pyramids

"Don't worry, it'll get worse..." More than Diana's novelty was wowing the world. Princess Grace–the original princess/star–was in a better position to understand a world addicted to Celebrity. Grace and Diana knew that while noble character whispers, pop-charisma explodes. Both had been brought up in immense privilege. But experience of a more real world, plus their street smarts and genuine warmth, ensured an affinity with ordinary people.

Windsor small talk was rendered insipid. We reporters ignored Charles when Diana plunged into walkabouts discussing morning sickness and dispensing hugs. Dilettante Charles made speeches about architecture. Diana adorably declared herself "thick as two short planks." The Prince and the Windsors tried to curb her meteoric rise but were outclassed. Diana parried with devastating skill. She had only to roller-blade in the park to knock Anne's good works off the front page. When Prince Charles scored the winning goal at polo, there was Diana rolling in the grass with her sons, effortlessly claiming magazine covers to make her more loved. Too late though, she realized privacy was the price. Once she had stepped through the looking-glass lens and beckoned the press into her private life, there was no turning back. We wanted to turn every aspect of Diana's existence into a royal Truman Show. When I visited Althorp a year after Diana died, I thanked Diana's brother, Charles, for opening his house (and his life) to the unblinking gaze of Di-trippers. "Heavens," he smiled, "It's only for two months[1] a year." His implication was clear. Scrutiny of his sister did not end when the gates clanged shut in fall. As Audrey Hepburn observed in *Roman Holiday*, it was "always open-season on princesses."

"I feel like Princess Di," grinned John F. Kennedy Jr, when assaulted by flash bulbs in New York. Even during their lifetimes, similarities between the Princess and the American patrician were clear. Both were young, beautiful, and adored beyond what is good for anyone. Both tried to master the engulfing media. He founded his magazine, she made a career out of controlling her public image. Ironically, both died in senseless accidents–their deaths brutal reminders that though societies anoint larger-than-life icons, these super-beings remain capable of the kind of poor judgment that brings squalid ends and shatters their perceived divinity.

In his grief, Diana's brother turned on the press. Lord Spencer accused those who profited from his sister of having "blood on their hands." He was naïve, of course. Paparazzi were beyond the pale but, for much of her career, the Princess enjoyed a symbiotic relationship with her regular accredited press. When confronting a foreign melee–in Argentina, 360 press people met her–we saw her eyes sweep the crowd, seeking the comfort of her familiar London followers. Leona Shanks also noted this vulnerability. "Some days there would be 60 reporters waiting for her outside our studio. Before she left, she would always pause and observe them through the window, to get a feel for the crowd. She felt a great comfort when she saw her 'regulars.' She thought if things got out of hand, they would protect her. She felt safe with them; there was an absolute comfort in their familiarity."

While Prince Charles had abolished meet-the-press parties, Diana resumed these tittle-tattle opportunities on her solo tours. We guzzled British embassy booze; she sipped Perrier and gossiped. Gazing from her goldfish-bowl life she was as interested in our soap opera as we were in hers. When a photographer contracted Delhi-belly, she sent her own physi-

The media response to Diana's pregnancies was as if no one has ever given birth before. A worldwide demand for royal maternity pictures is at last eclipsed by a craze for baby snaps. BELOW: William's first encounter with a gadget that will follow him all his life, the video camera.

1. The Spencer ancestral home in Northamptonshire welcomes the public between July 1 and August 31 each summer. Website is: www.althorp.com

TOP: A young Diana learns about the phenomenon of Celebrity from the original princess-superstar, Grace of Monaco.
ABOVE: Diana "obviously filled a void in the media's life that I had not filled," said disapproving sister-in-law Princess Anne.
BELOW: Author Susan Maxwell Skinner chats with Diana's brother, Charles Spencer, at Althorp.

JULIE NUNES

cian. She later asked the snapper, "which end was it coming out of?" I recall dropping my notes over the gallery rail in Parliament, New Zealand. The paper fell like ticker tape on the banquet below and I was sorely ashamed...until Diana beamed up at me with giggling eyes. At her press conference in Egypt, my friend photographer Anwar Hussein told Diana bartenders would not serve him because he was a Moslem. Knowing how he loved his wine, the Princess disappeared into the kitchen and returned with a glass for him. Photographer Jayne Fincher sobbed about missing pictures of the Waleses leaving hospital after Prince William's birth. "Well, I was crying, too," winced Diana. "I had just given birth and going down those stairs was so painful..."

At the time, 11 British daily newspapers were using her image to compete for readers. The encounters worked both ways. As the Wales marriage disintegrated, Diana choreographed images to demonstrate how ill used she was. The most graphic was turning her face from Charles when he attempted a kiss. As she intended, a hundred cameras recorded his humiliation.

Once she left her marriage behind, Diana used the press for altruistic purposes. She famously contrived images to champion unfashionable causes. Lepers and AIDS sufferers benefited. In the minefields of Angola and Bosnia, she treated her press followers as essential allies. "I hope," she told them, "that by working together we shall focus world attention on this...largely neglected issue." Anti-landmine treaties after her death might not have been signed without worldwide publicity for her crusades. Less virtuously, Diana found uses for the pack-hunting paparazzi. Weeks before her death, she pandered to camera motor drives at St Tropez. The bathing beauty knew something her stalkers did not. Her lovely body in next day's papers would ruin Camilla Parker Bowles' 50th birthday!

Early in the 90s, advancing technology called for faster newsbreaks and hotter celebrity gossip. As the biggest superstar on earth, Diana was an obvious bestseller. Her privacy diminished and London became as profitable for picture agencies as Los Angeles or New York. Having discarded police protection, she could go nowhere without a paparazzi pack. "You make my life hell!" she screamed as they blocked her car in traffic. Pictures stolen while she exercised in a gym brought about a retreat from public life. Paradoxically, this precipitated an open season. The paucity of fresh Diana pictures turned any outing by the Princess into a feeding frenzy. In tears, she told her hairdresser Sam McKnight about lens men who shouted four-letter taunts through her car window and snapped her appalled reaction. "She felt she had been raped daily," said McKnight.

But a uniform attitude to privacy was not possible with Diana's constant need for favorable PR. One day she might profess a wish to abandon public duties and be alone. The next, she might leak her movements or collude in a tell-all book. Her relationship with the press was a daily barometer of how much she wanted to help a charity or where she stood in her war with the Palace gray-guard. A typical star, she wanted to control what was printable and what was not. Her friend Lord Palumbo said: "She wanted (publicity) on her own terms...to use the press as she wanted. We all know it doesn't work that way." With the media as an accelerant, Diana had risen to super-stardom. In turn, newspapers often adopted a parental tone to scold the willful child they had raised.

In his speech at Diana's funeral Charles Spencer alluded to a media quest "to bring her down because genuine goodness (threatens) those at the opposite end of the moral spectrum." With Diana and her press, nothing was so black and white. Through their 17-year coexistence, Diana and journalism used each other with equal self-interest. At last, exhausted by the monster she had created, the Princess talked about leaving England to escape scrutiny.

Which she did. Not the way she planned but in the only way possible.

RIGHT: In the minefields of Bosnia and Angola, humanitarian Diana courted press people as allies. Said the activist: "By working together we shall focus world attention on this issue." LEFT AND BELOW: Take aim, fire! A press army (including the author and photographer) waits hours for a scheduled Diana appearance.

Charles Spencer spoke of Diana's "mischievous sense of humor and the laugh that bent (her) double."

CHAPTER EIGHT

The Comic Relief

"Don't say I'm sweet. I'm a normal person and I love life!"

—DIANA, BEMOANING HER GOODY-GOODY PRESS IMAGE, 1981.

Everyone remembers the tragic end. People tell you exactly where they were when they learned Diana was dead. I was at a country club wedding in Sacramento. A friend heard the news on his car radio and told me. I screamed aloud. How could Diana be stone cold and people still be partying on? Word filtered out. Soon a bridesmaid announced, "Princess Di just died in some drunk-driving accident." She was right. No conspiracy theory negates evidence that the al Fayed chauffeur had three times the legal limit of alcohol in his blood. But it was interesting that I instinctively defended Diana. "Diana does not drink," I snarled at the poor bridesmaid.

My journalist's instinct to salvage a botched story came back. So even as I watch—for the 20th time—video of Diana's exit from the Ritz Hotel in Paris, rationality vanishes. When the film rolls, I feel this tragedy can yet be averted. After all, there she is, rosy-cheeked and alive. She bursts through the revolving door...I recognize that long-legged stride. She still has four minutes to live. I really feel this time someone can stop her...

Today, I don't think of Diana in terms of the tragedy that ended her life. I prefer to recall an amazing, long-running pop opera with a cast of thousands and buckets of comedy. Instead of mourning her, I take Charles Spencer's advice and remember the magic. He spoke of her "wonderfully mischievous sense of humor and the laugh that bent (her) double." I saw plenty of that. For all her lack of formal education, she was a bright, funny person. In 16 years of celebrity, Diana gave relatively few speeches. Few interviews were made public. So only a handful of people felt the thrust of her humor. But after years of scrambling behind Diana—and talking to people she knew—I came to know what tickled her. I heard how wry, how self-effacing and even scathing the Princess became in order to survive the Windsor school of hard knocks. At the beginning of her public career, journalists delighted in calling her 'sweet.' Fifteen years later, Henry Kissinger described her as "a wonderful person with a very wicked sense of humor." She came in like Mary Poppins and went out a Joan Collins.

"Honestly, if I'd had my nose done, do you think I would have chosen *this* one?"

"People tend to ask extraordinarily personal questions..."

"Harry is always asking me to have another baby...he seems to forget that I have to be married first..."

Here are some Dianaisms on ...

BEING A MOTHER

- "If men had babies, they'd only have one each..." to a Birthright Charity Officer, 1984.
- "Charles came in (during Prince William's birth) and I kept saying: Charles, come here and hold my hand but he kept wanting to go to the front of the engine..." to her hairdresser, 1996.
- "Ooh, I want to bite his botty–I shouldn't say that, should I?" praising baby William's skin, 1982.
- "On (William's first birthday) I smiled myself stupid. The press was quite determined to see a 'sad mama'..." telling a friend about missing William's first birthday during her Canadian tour, 1983.
- "Harry is always asking me to have another baby. But he seems to forget that I have to be married first..." to a journalist, 1997.
- "You must be joking. I'm not on a production line..." when asked if she were again pregnant, 1982.
- "Charles knows so much about rearing children that I've suggested he has the next one. I'll just sit back and give advice..." to a friend, after William's birth, 1982.
- "William will be able to play with his canoe in the bath, if I'm not successful with these fishing flies, I can play with them in the bath as well..." receiving a toy canoe and fishing flies in Canada, 1983.
- "Harry is always teasing William: 'If you don't want to be king, it doesn't matter, I will be...'" to a journalist, 1997.
- "I can't stand being away from (Charles) in case I lay my egg. Wouldn't it be much easier, sitting on the nest, so I could vanish and then return to sit on my egg? The feathered birds have obviously got it all organized..." to a friend while expecting Harry, 1984.)
- "She said: 'At least he hasn't got his father's ears...'" recalling the Queen's first sight of Prince William, 1982.
- "I don't know what my mother-in-law would say if William had that done..." learning that a friend's son had a navel stud, 1997.
- "There is more to being a king than having a good serve..." when singer Cliff Richard praised Prince William's tennis, 1996.
- "I call them the killer Wales..." explaining William and Harry's love for hunting, 1996.

ROMANCE (AND DIVORCE) WINDSOR-STYLE

- "My first screen kiss..." retiring from the Palace balcony on her wedding day, 1981.
- "I thoroughly recommend it..." speaking of marriage to reporters, 1981.
- "It's all right, I'm a married woman..." accidentally entering the men's showers on the royal yacht Britannia, 1981.
- "Will my husband think I am sexy in this?" To maternity fashion designer Jasper Conran, 1984.
- "Really, my husband's such a child. Honestly, it's as if I had three little boys..." to secretary Patrick Jephson, 1992.
- "I see you've brought your other half. I left mine at home watching telly..." to singer Cilla Black, 1981.
- "George Michael's gay? What a waste..." to her hairdresser, 1997.
- "All men are bastards. Sorry Patrick..." to Patrick Jephson, 1994.
- "Who is getting the benefit of your wisdom today, the sheep or the raspberry bushes?" To Prince Charles in his Highgrove garden, 1985.
- "But at least he *earned* his medal..." when Charles said his aide had only one decoration, 1986.
- "I call these my Charles and Camilla shoes..." Pointing to the double-C Chanel logo, 1994.
- "Charles owes me a lunch..." offering her credit card to friends in a restaurant, 1994.
- "There were three of us in this marriage, so it was a bit crowded..." during a BBC interview, 1995.
- "I have the best mother-in-law in the world..." to a journalist, 1996.
- "After all I've done for that f*****g family..." to her friend James Gilbey, 1992.
- "Oh, do you think divorce agrees with me?" To fashion designer Arnold Scaasi, 1997.
- "Charles makes a great ex-husband..." letter to a friend, 1997.
- "I haven't taken such a long time to get out of a bad marriage to get into another one..." quizzed on marriage plans, 1997.
- "It'll go on the third finger of my *right* hand..." when told Dodi al Fayed might give her a ring, 1997.

BEING PRINCESS OF WALES

- "I would love to be a successful dancer...or maybe the Princess of Wales..." a prophetic joke, 1980.)

"I can never resist a good looking man in Armani..."

- "My father always told me never to talk to strangers and I've spent the last 15 years doing nothing but…" after being mobbed at a Sydney luncheon, 1996.
- "Oh, how strenuous…" at a ribbon-cutting, 1994.
- "I'm on holiday. Don't call me Princess. Just call me Diana…" to a young Belgium friend, Barbuda, 1996.
- "I would swap places with you any time…" to an Australian housewife, 1983.
- "A lot of tiara functions, which have left the head sore…" writing home from the Canadian tour, 1983.
- "People tend to ask extraordinarily personal questions and I tend to answer them with a blush…" same tour.
- "I always thought it was the wife first. Stupid thought…" when Charles served the Queen, the Queen Mother and, lastly, Diana, 1981.
- "It's not the dogs I don't like. It's the corgis. They get blamed for all the farts…" when asked about the royal dogs, 1995.)
- "It's really an outing for my husband. He gets to meet all his old rellies. Half the Royal Family's German…" discussing a trip to Germany, 1994.
- "Yuck, the flying tumble-drier…" contemplating a helicopter ride, 1987.
- "Another episode in the everyday story of royal folk…" alighting from the same helicopter.
- "I'm queuing! It's wonderful! You meet so many different people in a queue…" while disguised, on jazz club date with Hasnat Khan, 1996.
- "I won't have to pay for it, will I?" When offered a program for a charity gala, 1983.

"A lot of tiara functions, which have left the head sore…"

PEOPLE WHO STEP OUT OF LINE

- "The word is slim. My husband prefers me this way…" when told by a hat maker that she was thin, 1981.
- "You cheeky bastard…" when rugby player Will Carling suggested she looked less than great at the gym, 1993.
- "Thanks, I'll change it…" after a staffer said her hat looked 'very royal', 1988.
- "Don't even start. You're Latin. You know what a summer romance is all about…" to Argentinean friend who quizzed Diana about the Dodi al Fayed romance, 1997.
- "That's the best chat-up line I've heard…" when a young man invited her to play bingo, 1996.
- "You are supposed to shake hands, you know…" when a bystander kissed her, 1983.
- "Now, now, back to your basket…" to a cheeky dressmaker, 1981.
- "I'll make the jokes, thank you Patrick…" when her secretary attempted to be witty, 1995.
- "Hmm, we'll see about them…" when a fashion house gleaned much publicity from her patronage, 1981.
- "Quite right, too…" when a child refused to shake her hand, Brixton 1984.
- "I warn you, if you kiss my hand, you'll never live it down…" to a gallant schoolboy, 1981.
- "You bought these from your expense accounts, I presume…" to reporters who gave her flowers, 1981.
- "I thought you would all be in Mustique with Prince Andrew…" to London cameramen during Andrew's infamous Caribbean holiday with actress Koo Stark, 1982.
- "I cringed when he did that…" when airline owner Richard Branson put his arm around her shoulders during an Airbus launch, 1995.
- "I have visions of you lying on the pavement, looking up my dress…" when a reporter wrote about her underwear, 1984.

"I warn you, if you kiss my hand, you'll never live it down…"

"If men had babies, they'd only have one each..."

"So many men, so little time..."

FOOD AND HER LOOKS

- •"Lobster? Can we afford it?" Planning the menu for her first dinner party, 1981.
- •"Tonight finds us eating lobster. It's about the sixth to date. Yuck..." writing from the Canadian tour, 1983.
- •"Bloody lucky prawn..." when a prawn lodged in her cleavage, 1992.
- •"I hope you like chicken. I'm afraid we seem to eat a lot of it..." lunching with a new secretary, 1987.
- •"Just think, Nicholas Soames can eat all the food they've brought for me. I'd probably only have sicked it up anyway..." declining her husband's dinner party, 1995.
- •"I never drink alcohol. There's been too much of it in my family..." to a hairdresser, 1997.
- •"I was halfway asleep and I couldn't find my mascara. I'd never let anyone see me without my mascara. I'd rather be blown up..." to her hairdresser, after failing to evacuate during a security alert at Kensington Palace, 1997.
- •"I find riding horses only exercises the horse's legs..." when told she should ride for fitness, 1981.
- •"I have bruises all over my bottom..." telling garden party guests how children mobbed her, 1981.
- •"I used to have lots (of bosom) up top. Well it's all gone now that I've had my boys..." to journalists, 1987.
- •"Honestly, if I'd had my nose done, do you think I would have chosen *this* one?" When rumored to have had plastic surgery, 1986.
- •"Wearing a paper bag would be just fine..." discussing how she would *not* upstage the bride at a wedding, 1996.

"I never drink alcohol. There's been too much of it in my family..."

"A girl can't have too
many designer bags..."

- " I look like a drowned rat. But I'm visiting the blind people next door. At least they won't notice..." during a rainstorm, 1991.

CLOTHES, JEWELRY AND MATERIAL POSSESSIONS

- "I've got Brenda's rocks..." receiving a tiara and necklace as wedding presents, 1981. (Brenda is an irreverent nickname for Elizabeth II.)
- "Gosh, I'm becoming a very rich lady..." beholding the jewels she received as wedding presents, 1981.
- "Clothes make the woman. I know they certainly helped make me..." Diana's writing, 1996.
- "Charles gave me a beautiful emerald and diamond ring, which I spend most of my time looking at in a stupid gaze..." admiring her Christmas present, 1981.
- "Wouldn't you like to drive my new tinted-glass BMW 750, complete with a princess?" to a relative of boyfriend Hasnat Khan, 1996.
- "Try it on, try it on!" offering her engagement ring to the Althorp housekeeper, 1980.
- "The other day I scratched my nose with my ring. It's so big–the ring, that is..." pre-wedding walkabout, 1981.
- "What, you've never had an Armani frock? You poor, underprivileged girl..." to her hairdresser, 1997.
- "A girl can't have too many designer bags..." giving the same hairdresser a Louis Vuitton purse, 1997.
- "Will Queen Mary's emeralds do?" When artist Nelson Shanks asked if she had a green necklace, 1994.
- "It's my reward for the years of purgatory with this f*****g family..." deciding to keep royal jewels after her divorce, 1996.
- "They're not getting *that* back..." showing a sapphire and diamond pendant to a portrait artist, 1995.

HER SHORTCOMINGS

- "I'll never be a Lord Snowdon, will I?" Exhibiting honeymoon snaps for a servant, 1981.
- "I was hopeless at maths and I never have understood the 24-hour clock..." to schoolchildren, 1982.
- "In spite of what my teachers thought, I did actually learn something (at school) though you'd never know it from my O-Level results..." visiting her old school, 1995.
- "Brain the size of a pea, I've got..." to schoolchildren, 1982.
- "My head may be large but there's not much in it..." during a fitting for a riding hat, 1982.
- "They can talk to me because I'm one of them..." visiting mental patients, 1995.
- "Stand by for a mood-swing boys..." to staff at Kensington Palace, 1992.
- "I feel much better now..." after dancing in the rain in the Kensington Palace garden, 1997.
- "Why don't you write a book? They'll say I'm the nutty princess and you're the nutty healer..." to her healer Simone Simmons, 1996.
- "I can never resist a good-looking man in Armani." after a long aprés-concert chat with pop singer Beeb Birtles, Melbourne, 1983.
- "So many men, so little time..." emblazoned on Diana's tee shirt, 1996.
- "I'm still thick up here (indicating her head) but I've got it down here (her heart)..." to the Archbishop of Canterbury, 1996.

"I look like a drowned rat. But I'm visiting the blind people next door. At least they won't notice..."

"I'm still thick up here (her head). But I've got it down here (her heart)..."

The mouse that roared.
A thin, pallid,
round-shouldered
Diana of '85 and
the muscular, 90s model.
Diana has become
Di-Xena, Warrior Princess.

CHAPTER NINE

The Final Act

"I am stronger than I look."

–DIANA, ON WALKABOUT IN ARGENTINA, 1995.

Twenty years after the Wedding of the Century, I rediscovered my dog-eared Order of Service from the ceremony. I read the Victorian hymn a Northamptonshire teenager chose for her wedding and remembered how the words had moved me, a lifetime ago, in St Paul's.

"I vow to thee my country[1]–all earthly things above–
Entire and whole and perfect, the service of my love.
The love that asks no questions; the love that stands the test.
That lays upon the altar, the dearest and the best.
The love that never falters, the love that pays the price.
The love that makes undaunted, the final sacrifice."

The words told me that this 19-year-old high school dropout was no lightweight. She had a clear sense of the duties ahead. "The service of my love"–not just to a husband but also to the Commonwealth–was no idle promise. Sixteen years later, I heard the same hymn at her funeral. The lyrics were even more poignant. I realized Diana had fulfilled every promise.

It was hard to imagine we were burying 'Shy Di,' the terrified, blushing girl I met at a polo match just before her wedding. As her coffin passed Buckingham Palace, the Queen and a subdued gathering of royal highnesses bowed their heads to the woman they had stripped of her royal title a year before. The grief and the eulogies of the world suggested a Joan of Arc lay in that massive coffin. How Diana changed in those 16 years! World leaders no longer gushed about her lovely eyes. Nelson Mandela praised her as a champion for "the sick and the needy throughout the world." Margaret Thatcher felt "a beacon of light had been extinguished."

A light in people's lives, Diana brings cheer
ABOVE: To London hospital patients.
BELOW: With a shared bouquet
in Washington DC.

Diana's face and haute-couture wardrobe were no longer an issue. President Bill Clinton praised her "for ending the scourge of landmines." Where was the scholastic flop who once told her hat maker: "My head may be big but there's not much in it"?

The Princess of Wales had wrought her own miracle. She had transformed an insecure clotheshorse of the 1980s into a person eulogized–not quite as a saint–as one of the most influential people in history. In the years since, the world has not stopped discussing the woman Camilla Parker-Bowles dismissed as "that pathetic creature." The mouse had roared. At her death, all Britain forgot its stiff upper lip and wept openly. And the House of Windsor would never be the same.

Take a photograph of Diana circa 1981. Compare it

---

1. I Vow to Thee My Country, by Cecil Spring Rice.

to Diana snapped in the last year of her life. Remember her flighty ways with Fergie, Duchess of York–both of them poking umbrellas into bums at the Ascot races? Then think of Diana in pinstripes at podiums, de-stigmatizing HIV or eating disorders. Or, sans-lipstick, lobbing a grenade against arms dealers in 1997. Here was the Barbie Doll who alienated the Palace, defied the Establishment and became Di-Xena, Warrior Princess.

In her mid-30s, Diana did more than cut her hair and de-clutter her wardrobe. She got serious. The Times of London began to write about her–serious stories about serious works–as often as the tabloids did. Despite her ever-tangled love life, her addiction to astrologers, gymnasia and colonic irrigation, the woman formerly known as HRH was no longer a frivolous subject. She popularized marginal causes, insisting that HIV-Aids patients be hugged, 'untouchables' touched and landmines banished. "My God, I've had to grow," Diana observed.

The big hair and fussy clothes were gone. She had kicked her binge-and-purge eating pattern, built up her body and gained at least 15 pounds. She was strong and confident. You could hear it in her voice. When first I spoke to Diana years before, her words spurted out in a juvenile gush. But taking microphones at the age of 35, her voice was part Emma Thompson, part Margaret Thatcher. She chided people's prejudices. She showed anger and tears. Hinting at her own troubles, she made her speeches relevant to causes she supported. When Diana empathized with bulimics, anorexics and families in crisis we knew she had been there.

ABOVE: They look like an odd couple but humanitarian mentor, Mother Theresa of Calcutta, tells Diana: "We are both working for God."
BELOW: After intense vocal tuition, Diana emerges as a powerful speaker. De-cluttered, she adopts the Jackie Kennedy power-suit as a working uniform.

Finding her voice did not come easily or cheaply. She paid for 240 hours of private voice tuition. Actor and voice coach Peter Settelen[1] once saw Diana make a wimpy speech. She was "nervous and gauche, emphasizing all the wrong words with a very thin, little girl voice." He gave his critique to Diana's fitness trainer and was immediately invited to Kensington Palace. Settelen told me his client had "no self-confidence. She had spent years being lied to by all the people around her (about) Charles and Camilla. It was a wall of silence. Just like when she was a child and her father did not talk about her mother."

Diana unlocked her voice with Settelen's vocal exercises–learning to breathe from the diaphragm and "expressing out her negative feelings." One enjoyable exercise was to shout every swear word she knew. "And she knew plenty," he laughed. "I tried to turn the energy that was hurting her into something powerful and positive. We had a deal. She would no longer bow her head. She would stand tall, and she was taller than I am! I knew if I could get her up in front of an audience, speaking more powerfully and passionately than she had done before, her confidence would increase by leaps and bounds. People would no longer treat her as a bimbo and they'd really start listening to what she had to say." Diana's speeches had previously been written for her. Now coach and student worked on making Diana's words actually sound like Diana. William and Harry sometimes sabotaged their videoed rehearsals. The boys used silly voices and rude noises to distract Mummy. One session ended in gales of laughter after William loudly and deliberately farted.

The woman who had muddled her groom's Christian names during her wedding vows would eventually address the likes of Henry Kissinger, Barbara Walters and General Colin Powell with ease. She even became brave enough

1. For information on Settelen's 1995 book, "Just Talk To Me" see website: www.settelen.com/justtalk.htm

to ad-lib when campaigning for cerebral palsy in New York. General Powell prefaced Diana's speech by bragging of an ancestral link to the Spencers through his Jamaican forebears. When Diana took the podium, she began: "Ladies and gentlemen and cousin Colin..." This was not only quick-witted. A British aristocrat who acknowledged kinship with an African American became queen of politically-correct hearts.

Diana spat her words like venom in her 1993 speech about eating disorders. Settelen had helped calm her nerves ahead of time: "Imagine you're a hooker," he said. "You've been there, you've done that and you're fine." After the event, she spotted him in Kensington. "She stopped the car, flung open the door, swung out her leg and said: "Not bad for a hooker, eh?'" Telephoning the teacher later, she was euphoric. "I really felt as though I expressed *me* for the first time..."

Marguerite Littman, founder of the Aids Crisis Trust, summed up the more assertive Diana in 1997. "She's more sure-footed now...very disciplined. She exercises. She gets up early. She's sensible. But it's not a boring sensible...she brings oxygen into the room. Most people take it out."

In the AIDS pandemic, as with a handful of other stigmatized issues she called "battered this and battered that", Diana found a cause to give her heart. "I am going to cut a very different path from everyone else," she predicted to biographer Andrew Morton. "I'm going to break away from this setup and go and help the man on the street. I don't like the glamorous occasions any more... I would much rather be doing something with sick people." She told her friend Rosa Monckton: "I want to walk into (a hospice or hospital) and feel that I am needed. I want to do, not just *be*."

The Rev. Tony Lloyd, director of the Leprosy Mission, remembers an incident on the Zimbabwe-Mozambique border. "There were streams of refugees coming over the hills. Diana spotted a woman leper too weak or faint to join the rest. I hadn't, and I was the expert. She went to help. There were no photographers, but it was a beautiful sight, Diana holding this woman's stump where once a hand had been in both her beautiful hands..."

The Princess had a new philosophy. Propped against a statue of Jesus on her desk were these words, in her own writing: "You cannot comfort the afflicted without afflicting the comfortable." The insight she had gained in turning her own life around now drove Diana to help others.

"She was hugely compassionate," said Tony Lloyd of his patron. "Perhaps because she'd suffered so much rejection herself... she had an empathy for lepers who were cast out of their families." Her tenderness for HIV-Aids sufferers did much to promote compassion for them, years before other celebrities espoused the cause. She was pictured cuddling an afflicted child in New York in 1985. "No one in this country has ever done anything so symbolic for us," a hospital official said.

Before and after her death, the Princess was one of the most effective 20th Century figures in charity. "Diana used her power like a magic wand," said Debbie Tate, who worked with abused and HIV-positive children in Washington DC. "Everywhere she used it, there were changes, almost like a fairy tale." Hosting a dinner for the Hong Kong Cancer Fund, billionaire David Tang introduced Diana saying: "Your presence here today is like winning a lottery". In her last years Diana described her causes as "a good and essential part of my life. A kind of destiny." Charles Spencer immortalized her words on Diana's memorial 'temple' at Althorp: "Whoever is in distress can call me. I will come running, wherever they are."

It underscores the image transformation during Diana's last years that a woman–who had extra-marital affairs, spent a fortune on grooming, took Mediterranean holidays at the drop of a towel and died in the company of a

ABOVE: Touching you, touching me. "All people want to be touched. If you just reach out...the impact is extraordinary." A gloveless Diana visits 'untouchables' in India. BELOW: One of the poignant notes outside Kensington Palace, August '99.

S. SAMIOS

J. SKINNER

ABOVE: Diana's 'temple' beside the lake at Althorp. Nullifying suggestions of paganism, Charles Spencer mounted a cross on the Georgian folly. BELOW: The Queen and other royals bow their heads in respect as Diana's horse-drawn coffin passes Buckingham Palace. OPPOSITE: Lady of the lake. Althorp's island is a serene grave site. Says Charles Spencer: "Diana is in a place where no human being can ever touch her again..."

notorious playboy–could be seen as one of us. But as always with this leading lady, timing was everything. Her end came soon after she trudged through Bosnia, campaigning against landmines. So the final impression etched on public memory is not of a sybarite on a $32 million yacht. But of an activist humanitarian in chinos, caressing legless children.

Sometimes people ask me if Diana's humanitarianism was sincere. Or was it an elaborate substitute for the lack of love in her own life? It is a reasonable question; a cover girl among the destitute invites skepticism and I imagine the compassion she delivered demonstrated what she wanted for herself. But I am reassured by Mother Theresa's sincere affection for Diana. They seemed an odd couple. Dying days after the Princess, the nun had only her cotton sari to bequeath. Diana left about $53 million and a wardrobe that filled Kensington Palace. Mother Theresa eschewed publicity. Press attention was oxygen to Diana. Yet they were firm allies. The younger woman was buried with a rosary from Mother Theresa. Had Diana been a phony, I believe the humanitarian nun would have seen through her in a minute.

But she told Diana: "You know, you could not do my work and I could not do yours. We are both working for God." She described Diana's gift better than anyone: "You bring light to people's lives."

I often think about these words. I recall following Diana through hospital wards and seeing despondent people practically floating on the ceiling after she left. She had merely sat on beds, chatted and touched. Even Diana was staggered by this power. "It's amazing," she said. "All people want to be touched. If you just reach out your hand and let them touch you, the impact is extraordinary." On Diana's walkabouts people often burst into tears after meeting her. I never knew why. I suspect it had something to do with that gift of bringing light to people's lives. With a few words and the touch of her hand, she gave ordinary people a priceless gift. They would take to their graves the memory of a fabled princess who briefly treated them as though they were the most important person in her life. Once I saw a blind man complain he could not see her. Diana took his hand to her face and he traced her features.

Even in the most cosmetic way, just glimpsing Diana's smiling face on paper every morning did help set Britons up for the day. For more than 16 years, her smile was as much part of breakfast as toast and marmalade. The end of those entertaining years seems now like a modern rerun of *My Fair Lady*, when it dawns on Professor Higgins that–damn, damn, damn–he is *Accustomed to Her Face.* In the abrupt final act of Diana's tragi-comedy life, billions of people discovered they were not merely accustomed to Diana. They were addicted.

I visited Kensington Palace four years after Diana's death and read the tributes on her gates. Some were flowery. Some were maudlin and, some, still bitter. One read: "They'd like us to forget...but,

dear girl, we haven't, and we won't." A street poet got the legacy of pop heroism about right.

"That beautiful face
and all the good things you done in this world.
How can we ever forget you?
You was my Queen."

I am not the only one of Diana's former press team who still dreams of her. She was part of our daily lives for a long time and, I suppose, she haunts our sub-conscious. I encountered her, vividly alive, as I slept recently. She happily skated pirouettes on a frozen lake. Waking, I recalled seeing her dance in Sydney. She had spun around a glistening ballroom floor, eyes, hair and silver shoes shining. She was a magical being. She remains my fairytale.

I later told Diana's American friend Nelson Shanks about the skating dream. Could it mean that her final exploits were on thin ice? I asked.

"No Susan," the artist smiled. "It means she is happy. And she is free."

I truly hope so.

The Bit-Players

Author and speaker Susan Maxwell Skinner.

Born in New Zealand, Susan Maxwell Skinner joined her first newspaper at the age of 16. She worked her way to feature writing and eventually covered visits by Britain's Royal Family. A plum assignment—attending the Royal wedding in 1981–changed her career direction. The writer stayed on in London. She was accredited to cover day-to-day royal engagements and later, tours by the Prince and Princess of Wales and senior members of their family. Highlights of these years included seeing Prince William and Prince Harry's debuts and sharing exotic tours with their parents. *Diana, Memory of a Rose* is her third book on the Princess of Wales. Susan is now married to American bandleader, John Skinner. They live in Sacramento, California, where the author is active on the speaking circuit. She is also a professional big band singer and recording artist.

To contact Susan Maxwell Skinner, phone USA (916) 481-0334
E-mail   sknrband@aol.com

Anwar Hussein's spectacular photo library has catalogued world events and royal activities for more than 30 years. He developed an interest in photography in his native East Africa and later documented pop culture of 70s London with brilliant show business portraits. The emergence of Princess Diana heralded the busiest period in royal photojournalism. Through his years of travel with the Princess, Anwar Hussein's library is now one of the best pictorial sources for Diana's history. He has also produced books on other members of the Royal Family. Hussein's pictures have been published and exhibited all over he world. The photographer and his family live in Wiltshire, England.

To contact Anwar Hussein,
E-mail   ANWAR@HUSSEIN.DEMON.CO.UK

The Author and photographer
Anwar Hussein.

As a photojournalist team, Susan Maxwell Skinner and Anwar Hussein have collaborated
in three books and hundreds of magazine articles about Princess Diana.